My Heart in Hiding

I0203642

Mary T. Fisher, O. P.

My Heart in Hiding

Mary T. Fisher, O.P.

DOMINICUS BOOKS
Chandler, Arizona

My Heart in Hiding

All Rights Reserved © 2008 by
Mary T. Fisher, O.P.

No part of this book may be reproduced or transmitted in any form
or by any means, graphic, electronic, or mechanical, including
photocopying, recording, taping, or by any information storage
retrieval system, without the written permission of the publisher.

For information address:
Dominicus Books
c/o Robert Curtis, O.P.L.
P.O. Box 6331
Chandler, Arizona 85246
Printed in the United States of America
by www.lulu.com

ISBN 978-0-6152-0942-5

Dedicated

to those I love.

You know

who you are.

Acknowledging

❖ *the appreciation and encouragement of Regina Williams, O. P., whose support blessed me with confidence to begin this project;*

❖ *family members, especially my beloved sister Barbara, who has helped so much; friends and associates who bolstered me with prayer, patience, and hope;*

❖ *Martina Stegman, O. P., for permission to use her line drawings;*

❖ *Dominicans of St. Albert Province for the use of clip art;*

❖ *Microsoft Word and Office Online for use of clip art and photos;*

❖ *auteur, teacher, mentor, advisor, guide, Dominican Brother and friend Robert Curtis, who helped immeasurably;*

❖ *above all, the Racine Dominicans, to whom, after God and family, I owe everything.*

Table of Contents

Part One: *A Poetic Potpourri*

Part II: *What is God Like?*

Part III: Rockin' Chair Reflections

Part IV: Glimpse of an Addicted Woman

Part I:

A Poetic Potpourri

I'm not sure if these are poems;
some of them might be.
They are in no special order,
follow no specific theme.
If you don't like one,
try another.
I hope you enjoy
at least a few.

After 800 Years...

He strides freely, this Preacher Dominic,
Baptismal seal, a star brow- emblazoned,
Head held high, listening... listening...
Enveloped wholly in the Word of God;
For 800 years inspiring others to follow
Through fog'ged ambiguity, perilous paths
Courageously conquering contradictions' chasms,
Proclaiming passionately: trumpet-calls
To guard and pass the Torch of Truth.
Fire blazes in his heart, consumed
With love for God and souls.

Graciously dispensing Waters of Wisdom,
Dauntless Dominic, Doctor of Truth, teach us.
Rose of Patience, Tower of Chastity,
  Golden-tongued Preacher,
Light of the Church, illumine us.
You freely offered wondrous hope of heaven
 Fulfill your promise by your prayers .
 We, your children, beseech you:
 <u>Father</u> us unto Life and Love.

Sr. Jean Dorcy, D.P.

At My Mother's Bedside—1

Quietly, gently
She listens, lingers, loves
As she eases toward Eternity.
Devoted hearts and hands
Minister daily, surrendering her
Yet longing still to keep
All lent to us so graciously:
Her soul's strength,
Tenderness, and valor.
As she sleeps,
Slipping slowly from us,
We watch, whispering prayers,
Weeping our loss, yet sure in faith
Of a glorious re-birth
And renewal in Christ,
Whose resurrection is our hope.

At My Mother's Bedside—2

She loves us too much to say "Goodbye"
And leave. Lingering, tarrying yet a while,
 Her benedictions enfold us, her smiles
Still bless our days. Gently, tenderly,

She takes her leave with
Each morning's sigh,
Each evening's kiss.

Slowly, through silken shadows
She slips away
Toward Eternity.

We are the richer for
Her lengthy farewells.

Death in Autumn

To go Home in Autumn—what great joy!
Escaping bonds of time while Nature holds
Its annual rainbowed-beauty contest,

Tinting leaves in glorious hues;
As we   lovingly enfold
Fond memories of
Scarlet-tipped tree tops, blushing bush;

A grand farewell and bold:
Trumpet sound of vibrant color
Heralding **New Life In Heaven**,
While Autumn gilds earth gold.

Do Widzenia, Mamusia*

Till we meet again, dearest Mama

Ours was a special love.
We understood each other;
We cherished each other's soul.

Laughter and tears we shared—
Poetry and music and song.
Our hearts felt at home together—

Warmly welcoming, we drew
Both soft comfort and gentle strength
 From hearts' affections.

No one ever lost—
Because no one ever had—

      So much.

Loss

Throughout Nature's changes, I mourn my loss.
When pretty Princess Spring sprightly skips away,
Leaving lush Lady Summer unrivalled to reign,
I bid farewell to you once more,
Weeping through gentle rains, sighing breezes.

      Before long that lovely Lady graciously bows
      To brightly pied, deep-crimsoned Autumn.
      But much too soon he abdicates his throne
      While leaves, dejected, spin tumbling down.

Anew then breaks my heart, dark-dappled
 Yielding, like Earth, to barrenness, cold;
While frigid King Winter icicles my soul.

Merciful God, free Spring from her dark prison;
Grant warmth, life and love to my grieving heart!

Pilgrimage

Gulping yellow roadlines,

My chariot creeps along.

Trees steal past the windows;

Mountains meander, strong.

It crawls to my heart's haven

Where Love knows I belong.

Peace waits there to welcome—

Serene, with tranquil song;

I'll bless its easeful cadence.

But oh! the way stretches long!

Musings

Daydreams offer sweet,
healing balm
For the lonely,
heart-sick soul.
Let us dream, then,
and find solace in
Pastel butterflies
and sepia-tinted memories.

Diminished in mysteriously
varied ways,
What do we have now
but memories?
Cherish them;
hold them close.
They comfort and warm
our nights and days.

I meet you again,
hold you once more
in memories.

Children in Darfur

Their large dark eyes stir my soul;
Parched lips and swollen tongues
Whisper in voices louder than thunder,
Pleading, begging for help.

Huge bellies and shriveled limbs
Offer mute testimony to their agony.
What can I do; how can I make
A difference in their lives?

The trains bound for Auschwitz
Are loading again.
Can I just stand by
And watch....
And wail....
And weep?

At Darfur

Hear the mournful wailing of mothers,
The hiccupping sobs of children.
See arm bands of red, green, or white
Branding, slitting, slashing, shredding
Tenuous bonds of hard-won family unity.

In this cold world and dark,
How we need each other's love,
Warm, soothing comfort!

Come to my open arms, sisters, brothers.
I enfold you; lean on me,

Like a pelican of old, I offer myself:
Feed off me and my hope.

My heart is one with yours,
God and I embrace you.

Holy Communion

It lies nestled in my hand,
This white Host,
For precious seconds as we measure time.
During that infinitesimal moment,
Gazing at It, I firmly believe
Christ, whole and entire—
Body, Blood, Soul, and Divinity—
Rests sacramentally on my palm, and

I am Mary, Virgin-Mother,
Caressing her Newborn;

A sinner, clutching His robe;

Martha, preparing a meal,
Magdalene, bathing His dusty feet,
Veronica, wiping His dear, bloodied face.

I am myself, weak, needy, yearning
For union with Him.
"Come, Beloved, come!"
And kissing the Host, I receive Him.

Morning Prayers

Early morning fog slithers
Across my garden
As I carry a cup
To the back-porch swing.

There, coffee-flavored psalms and I
Greet God in the misty, murky dawn,
Singing Divine praises.

Our "Allelluia!" rouses the lazy sun
To send weak rays through the haze.
" An ordinary day," I think; but then
God delights me with a surprise;
A hummingbird flits by,
Wings whirr-whirr-whirring
As it sips nectar from blossoms.

Singing God's praises fills me
With sweetness, too.

Christmas

Trailing clouds of celestial glory,
God's Mighty Word eagerly leapt
Astounded pregnant darkness
To lonely fractured Earth
That Holy, Silent Night.

In serene stillness today again
He comes to our hushed hearts
Hungry for healing Love.

Quietly waiting, we worship now,
Whispering welcome to our God.

The Conqueror

God's love is a tenacious vine that curls around my heart;
Persistent tendrils creep into my soul's innermost crevices,
Twining between, above, under, beneath and over
            iron-clad indifference.

Tender shoots twist through secret hideaways,
Infiltrating, usurping stubborn squatters there,
Enfolding, possessing me irretrievably, triumphantly.

Slowly, over many years, though I resist His reign,
My grudging acquiescence is transformed to
Tremulous abandonment, flaming love;
And I beg God to grow and bloom within me.

To a Lost Love

Somewhere it's springtime.
Swollen seeds sprout, buds burst,
Shy smiles burgeon, too.

Somewhere it's springtime:
Robins sing, roses bloom,
Skies are ever blue.

Somewhere it's springtime—
Rain's but a soft mist
Sunshine filters through.

Somewhere it's springtime
With music and laughter,
And all the world's new.

Somewhere it's springtime--
There MUST be a springtime!—
And somewhere there's you

At Emmaus

Nearing its mystic goal is the journey I started alone.
Along the paths, I marvel: swiftly the years have flown!
 Companions, friends, have eased my way by caring,
By loving words of comfort, remembering, and sharing.

O'er rugged roads, craggy steeps, fields of velvet green,
Waters rough or silky smooth : splendid sights I've seen
Yet through it all, a yearning ache, a hunger dwelling
Within my restless soul, bereft beyond all telling.

In broken bread, and given : pierced hands extending
In Eucharistic, saving grace: Love's Sacrifice unending.
Searchings ceased at Emmaus; longing heart then knew:
Christ, You are my love, my life,   Journey ends in **You**.

 I recognize Your love, Lord, in Breaking of the Bread.
Please take my wayward heart and give me Yours instead.
Stretching Your arms in welcome, bring me to Your side;
My weary wanderings over, in You I now abide.

Sonnet to a Loved One:

M_ _M_

Because I love you so, I leave you free.
I shall not bind your heart by tears or touch
Or knowledge of my need, who love so much.
Unselfish, unconditional, may this love be.

Perhaps some day when pain or grief or cold
Assail your heart, my love may be a cloak
Warm around your weary shoulders, each fold
A tender comfort; or else a stalwart, sturdy oak

That lends its strength if darkling days appear.
When rainbows arch skies of cerulean blue,
In those glad times, as well, may I be near
To thank our God and share life's joys with you.

But, Dearest, never fear a cloying touch.
I leave you free. I love that much.

Pyrotechnics

Mysterious mists swirl above the waters;
Ghostly ribbons enshroud the horizon,
Eerily obscuring the gray shore.

Then suddenly, inexplicably!
Brilliant beams of light invade the gloom,
Exploding, bursting
Into radiant shards of color.

So may your dauntless Spirit, valiant God,
Expand the dull, hesitant horizons of my life;

Dissolve petty boundaries, limited vision,
Vibrantly piercing my pallid weakness.

Rainbow, Creator God, rainbow in me,
That I may bear witness
To Your
Kaleidoscopic love.

Spring Summons

All Earth gentles now:
Rough winds abate to balmy breezes;
Bare, dark starkness of winter limbs
Yields to softer silhouettes—

Lacy outlines fuzzily etched
Across cerulean skies.
Nubile buds swell in fields and fens,
Farms and forests.

In my heart, too,
Spring whispers of hope and life.

While turtle-dove calls to its mate
And shy crocus tentatively peek
From greening beds,

My Lover gently calls me to rebirth,
Burgeoning of spirit, to
Fuller life in Him.

Gustatory Delights

John Keats exulted in nectarine's lushness
        sluicing down his chin;
"Mmmmm," moans Marcie, her mouth melting
        with chocolate's dark magic;
Tommy smacks lips deliciously dripping
        with ice-cream seeping through sticky fingers...

(Taste— and see the goodness of the Lord.)

Within my soul I taste you, my God.
 You are honey to my lips,
Sweetness to my spirit;
Richness to my palate.

I taste, I savor you, for you satisfy
 My hunger,
Thirst, and
Infinite desire.

Snowflakes

They tell us no two are alike—snowflakes, I mean.
Well, no two of **us** are alike, either.
Each one uniquely, marvelously made.
No one can love God the way I do;
No one can give honor, glory, praise
As I can; no one's life can mirror God
Exactly the same way MINE can.

Help me to be really myself and
 True to my hopes, dream, aspirations,
 Merciful God of all creation.
Teach me to offer you humbly
Gifts no other creature can:
 My own specialness, uniqueness.

 In the compassionate fire of your love
 Burn away the dross, purify the ore
Until only precious metal remains—
Rare gold of my being.
 Help me to believe in myself,
 To treasure You-in-me,
 To rejoice that I am the only one of my kind,
 Your very special snowflake.

Basic Catechism Questions

Who loves me so much that he carefully
counts every hair on my head?
Who strengthens my weak, fragile spirit
with comforting words he has said?

Who batters and begs for admission
to my shuttered and selfish heart?

Who has promised his presence forever,
through all my fair days and dark?

Who welcomes me home, forgiving
each time I have foolishly strayed?

Who patiently, graciously listens
to every request I have made?

I know the answer, dear God—
It's you!

Aubade

(a morning song)

Toes curl, then spread, squishing
      gritty, dew-dampened sand.
I dance the dawn-kissed sea-shore,
      while turquoise-tinted waves
Beat against stolid rocks
      in metronomic measure.

Distant white-caps frolic
      in rhythmic abandon.
Exuberantly giddy birds
      swoop and sway,
Trilling their morning greeting
      to the primrose-pink sun.

Together we praise Him
      Who fathers forth such beauty.

Serenade

(evening song)

Under a raspberry-ruffled sky, lavender-laced,
Tranquility wraps me 'round:
Whisper-soft, calming comfort.

Impatient spirit settles, serene now;
Anxious heart Spirit-healed at seashore.

Yesterday's worries seep into the sand,
And tomorrow's fears melt, washed away.

Only the present matters: **now**, this instant,
Already past as I name it.

Distant horizons bloom, limitless,
Offering rosy hope: Acceptance.

Let Mystery be. No answers needed.
Trust waits, at peace with Possibility,
Enfolded in the loving arms of God.

Anatomy of a Depression

The following poems about my bouts with depression are extremely personal. They are offered here with the hope that others may read, understand, and be supported by the knowledge that they are not alone, and that help is available—sometimes just around the corner.

I

That early morning when Mom died

Lights went out for Dad,

Never to come on again.

For two long years he lingered,

Captive in a bleak world

Without fresh air or flowers

Or tasty food—

Endless nights without dawnings,

Dark, lost, and alone...

Now I know how he felt.

II

My heart has turned to gray powder

Moldering in a musty box.

I shake it once in a while

To see if anything happens.

Nothing does, so

I return it to its creaky shelf,

Companioning dusty dreams,

Faded hopes, and

Memories' blurred silhouettes.

III

An inchworm, I crawl towards death,
Dragging my heavy spirit
Over endless terrain.
Why bother? Too much...
Too much...too much ennui,
Frustration and pain.

IV

No, I won't kill myself.
I want to <u>live,</u> not die.
But is this life—this heavy grayness
With ease found only in sleep's
Blanketing comfort? Am I alive,
Or have I already begun
An easeful, empty, lonely death?

V

I lie here helpless, inert.
No reason to rise, to greet the day
With melancholy murmurs.
Can't I just stay here and disappear,
Waste away to nothingness, already
Claiming my spirit? I long
Only for dissolution and vacuum. Leave.
Leave me. Leave me alone. Alone.

VI

Frozen in mid-leap,
All gravity suspended, I
Can neither safely land nor fly.
Caught here, perilously air-borne,
I quiver and shiver and sigh.

VII

I clutch my pain closely to me
Like a lover, not proven enemy.
Why prod a tooth that keeps on aching?
Why nudge a heart that insists on breaking?
Victim and victimizer—both am I.
Better to sleep, to dream, to die.

VIII

A fearful, frantic mole,
I gamely dig toward light,
 Then stop.
What if it's another illusion?
At least here it's safe, warm,
Though dark.

IX

If I were truly depressed
Would I be editing,
Conscious of metaphors,
Careful of spelling, punctuation?
Perhaps I'm only a Drama Queen,
Self-absorbed, warmly cocooned
Against reality, isolated, aloof.
All right. Help me change, please.
Give me a catechism to memorize,
Exercises, rituals to practice.
What is the Decalogue Against Depression?

X

Incapable of lofty thoughts,
Pleasing phrases,
I come before you
In depression's rags
With a mouthful of moldy ashes.
Behold me, God,
Tattered and mute.
Please accept this bundle
Of nothingness
With my rueful regrets,
With my late-blooming love.

"1600 Insurgents Killed"

Scream the headlines,
Boasting of lives taken.

Stunned, staggering, fearful,
 1600 men, women, children
Die, moaning in agony.

3200 eyes forever closed to beauty,
3200 arms and legs immobile
3200 feet with no place to go;
1600 voices silenced,
1600 hearts stilled.

"1600 Insurgents Killed."

They didn't know they were "insurgents."

They just wanted to
Love and laugh and live
A little longer—

Just like us.

Invitation From a
Grumpy Old Woman

Please--
Stop the impatient click-clack of heels
Tempt me to friendship.
Reach out:
Bless me with a touch—
Not as magnetized shavings,
Not as birds a-skim,
But as sisters.
Peer behind rheumy eyes,
See beneath parchment skin,
Folds of fat or skeleton-frame
And wrinkles.
Entice me to wholeness.
Love me into loveableness,
Stir me to life again,
Please?

Lover-God,

Today I feel helpless as a child,
Lost, uncertain, faltering-- alone
In an icy wilderness.

Rescue me, I humbly beg you.
My own resources have withered,
Leaving me destitute, frozen.

Come to me, God of my heart,
Please restore me to life.
Wrap me 'round with your mercy;
Enfold me in the warmth
Of your boundless love.

Consume me in the flame
Of your burning passion.
Claim me as your own.
I am yours. Take me.

Unheard Music ?

Middle Ages gravely pondered "Music of the Spheres."
Moderns marvel at whales' mating-calls, dolphins' cries;
Computers fashion tunes from heart beats or exotic
      rhythmic patterns.

Why may not my soul sing melodies too dear for sound
As I contemplate God, my Beloved; as I tell of my love.

Songs welling from my depths have no words,
Chant in no heard melody.
But they rise O! so sweetly!

Exultant, soaring notes stretch yearningly to Him
      Whom I seek,
Whom I love with passion ardent as a bride's.

Embrace me, my God; take me—I am yours.
Let us sing our duet in heavenly harmony...
A descant of divine desire.

Plea

Even in its last quarter
The tired, gray moon
Reflects light
And shares Beauty.
So too, Lord,
May I ?

ShShShhhhhhhh

Moon-lit leaves tremble,
Awe-struck, hushing in the silence:
"God is here.
Be still."

Mother Love: a Sonnet

Together with my sisters, I have known
Mystic labor pains, then glorious birth;

In fertile fields or rocky roads I've sown
Seeds of faith, and tended burgeoning earth.

Spirit-blessed, humble nurturing powers
Have crowned with fruit abundant joy and tears.

Today, past youth, in slower, silent hours,
My listening heart, on eager tiptoe, hears

Christ's call: "Live for My Church, fecund and free
To <u>mother</u> searching, lonely sheep and lamb";

With woman's warm compassion e'er to be
Proclaiming **love** by all I have and am.

No need have I for fruitless, fond regret:
Baptismal oils still seal, anoint me yet.

Jubilees

We remember your Jubilees, dear Sisters and friends:
Dedicated decades, swiftly flown years

Faith-burnished in ministry, brightened by prayer,
Sparkling with laughter, hallowed by tears.

Happy your Jubilee! We now acclaim
Your peaceable presence, heart-touching grace,

As quietly serving, blessing, healing,
Generously giving, you showed us Christ's face.

Glorious your Jubilee—radiant with joy,
Exultantly celebrate! Gleaming, ablaze

Your love of Creator, Redeemer, and Spirit—
For God-centered years, we rejoice and sing praise!

Winter Wonder

Who spares a passing glance

At sere and frozen oak leaves,

Ice-crystalled in *locus*—

Till suddenly—

Before the eye can focus:

Crocus!

Ready, March !

Untouched by the greening mist of spring,
Branches hold themselves rigidly attentive--
Soldiers inflexible, unbending,
Patiently waiting for Nature's command
To mellow with springtime's sweetness.

Spring Rain

I seed the white, sugar-candy clouds
With my dreams,
Entrusting them to sunshine,
Hoping for fruition.
Instead, they fall as
Dreary, teary rain.

Careful--!
Lest you step
In a puddle
Of my watery,
Wastrel dreams.

Poverty of Spirit

Poor in spirit am I, Lord,
Lacking power even to lift my head
To praise You.

Poorly clad in tattered rags I hobble,
Unfit for fine robes,
Unworthy to be in Your presence;
Robbed of speech, I am dumb, voiceless,
With punctured dreams, faded hopes;
Betrayed by empty promises from straw-
            filled scarecrows.

Nothing but empty-handed failure
In my larder...and great, abiding
Need of You, my God.
Hungry, thirsty for Your love, I am
Too poor to bargain, ashamed to lift my
            eyes.
I count on Your great mercy alone.

Take me, Lord: I beg of You.
Have pity on my poverty and
Make me rich in You.

Soul's Music

Life sings soft, simple songs
      for those who love,
Blending harmonies in tonal counterpoint,
Lifting lilting descants to soar
      above melodic lines.

But discordant loss distorts
      each yearning phrase,
Souring notes and wrenching rhythms,
Jarring joyful modality
To minor melancholy.

Return to lift my heart once more,
God of music and harmony;
Grant peace to this wayward,
Wanton, willful one.
Put love in order in me.

December Snow

Drop gently, snow, upon the tired earth;
Drift softly, snow, this season of His birth.

Fall sweetly, snow, blanketing the ground;
Ermine-cover, snow, with never a sound.

Work deeply, snow, earth's dark core within;
Till springtime proves the blessing you have
       been.

Through hectic nights, frenetic days
Your silence speaks of calming, peaceful ways.

Please teach me, God, the lessons I can know
Taught by the quiet, gentle, gracious snow.

Final Vows

I pledge no prudent, cautious love,
Shy, reluctant to name itself.
My love leaps in joyous abandon:
Bold banners billowing,
Scarlet ribbons streaming,
 Framed in fireworks and flashing starlight.
Articulate—Oh yes!—with arms spread
Wide in wildly welcoming embrace,
Coming--finally—**home**
To celebration, song, and you.

Ring of Love

Love sanctifies the ground it stands on;
Music breathes through the mystic air.
Hearts intertwine, meld, become one:
No sure beginning or end
Apart from the other: a circle, symbol
Of God's Love, eternally transforming,
Unchangeably true.
Marvel, reverence, and venerate
Every blessed place where love dwells.

Mutiny

Who do you think you are—
Breaking into my heart this way,
Pillaging, plundering with impunity,
Riding rough-shod over frail emotions,
Battering down admittedly feeble defenses?
Did I relinquish privacy, every paltry privilege?
Can't I cling to anyone, anything, anymore?
By what right do you stake such certain claim
On my faltering love, my timid allegiance?

Must I grant each outrageous request
With no recourse against your random rummaging?
What do you want with me, anyway—
Weak, hesitant, stumbling as I am?
Why should I now meekly trust you,
Cede to daring, divinely demented demands?
Who do you think you are,

My God.

Pain

Pain and I are old friends,
Understanding, accepting familiar foibles
For the sake of good found in each other.
Sometimes her piercing sharpness
Surprises me breathless;
But I forgive her bold insistence,
And she overlooks my naiveté.

Reminding me of mortality in her
Nocturnal visits, she often hears
My resentful murmurs.
But, friend-like, she forgives.
Occasionally, she wraps me 'round in
Compassionate numbness.
Grateful for her easeful care,
With trembling lips I bless her;
Then I rest, at peace with pitying Pain.

But today I can't help wishing
She would find another friend and release me,
Just for a little while.

In the Chapel at Guest House

(Dedicated to all who pray there)

Through panes of delicately tinted glass—
Palest yellow, soothing lavender, peaceful green—
I glimpse bare branches soaring straight and true,
Stretching heavenwards
Past skies leaden and gray.
Deep within their centers sleepily stirs life,
Waiting to waken and fructify.

Deep within my center, too, stir drowsy dreams—
Timid, afraid, uncertain,
Yet yearning for fulfillment,
Longing for signs of vibrant life,
Renewed hope, serene happiness.

Come, God of all Beginnings and Endings,
And all that lies between;
Melt my ice-crystalled winter heart;
Inflame it with Your springtime love.

Happy Anniversary

How smoothly roll the words,
But how ruggedly rough the road, traveled
Through years of sacrifice and struggle.

No matter now the pain or wounds;
Heartaches, headaches pale before
Countless victories;
Dreams reclaimed, lives regained, hopes
re-flamed.

Question the ones
Whose shadowed lives have been forever
changed
Through your unselfish ministry;
By your loving, anointed hands
Raised in blessing and service.

Eyes now bright with hope, triumphant
They stand, unfettered by
Fear, failure, or faceless dread,
Offering grateful testimony today
To glad cause for celebration.

Tango Time ?

When a samba beat
Seduces my feet
I'm in a <u>dancing</u> mood.

I waltz with wafting breezes,
Schottische to the stars.
A graceful minuet will do
'Twixt Venus, Earth, and Mars.

Oh, don't pin down my spirit;
Unfettered let it be;
Pirouetting as I polka,
Terpsichorially free.

Like a feather, a firefly, a fancy,
I'm in a dancing mood!

Sea Voyage

Embrace each swelling wave
That roils across Life's sea;
Its surging,
Churning turbulence
Need not perilous be:
For Christ stands at the helm
Beside you
With Mary there to guard
And guide you
Past shallow shores,
Desolate deeps;
Shadowed shoals,
Rugged reefs,
Triumphantly to conquer
Even darkest night.
Their love and grace support you
As your ship sails toward the light.

Memory's Moments

I don't remember days—
I remember moments:
Isolated instances
Flash like lightning
Through mists of the forgotten. . .
Piercing oppressive shadows,
Radiant memories gleam--
Glittering slivers of light
To illumine, warm, and cheer
A desolate heart.   Still and ever
It yearns for love long lost,
Found now only
In memory's magic moments.

Master Poet

I am a jumbled confusion of letters:
No meaning, no sense can there be.
No one can fathom or know how
To decipher the mystery of me.
But God is the Master Wordsmith.
Unraveling each tangled skein,
He unlocks the depth of my yearnings,
Unscrambling and making them plain.
He solves my puzzles, my riddles,
Inspiring with life-giving soul,
Infusing each phrase with His wisdom,
Sanctifying, gracing it whole.

Ply your craft, then, God-Wordsmith,
Take my words, take each fractured day;
From twisted enigmas bring beauty
In your own inscrutable way.

Compose of my life a great poem—
Compassionate, ordered, and true;
My conundrum life has meaning
Only, Wordsmith-God, in you.

Maid in-Waiting

Mary bloomed, skilled at waiting after her faith-filled "Fiat."
"Let it be done," she had said; sanctified serenity
 Sweetly cloaked her in peaceful expectation.
She bore Joseph's puzzled gaze in silent fidelity,
Calmly waiting for God's vindication.

Tranquilly she trod the questioning hill-country,
Quietly sheltering within her the Lord of Life.
Serene, she fulfilled the law's demands,
Heavily trudging toward Bethlehem's unknowing throngs.

Unfalteringly faithful, she fretted not at rejection,
But sank, grateful, upon a rude   stable floor
Where straw, beasts, and silence welcomed her.
Again she waited, graciously patient,
 For her world and ours to know cosmic change.

In Honor of St. Dominic

Dauntless Dominic, valiant Father, in apostle's role you came
Countering heresy with mercy, boldly preaching in God's name
With God's Word a flaming torch you zealously set world ablaze
Guiding others, quick to follow, how to bless, preach and praise.

Dominic, courageous champion of the Truth that sets all free,
Student of divine and human, counseling us ever to be
Faithful to the call compelling us to justice, peace, and love:
Contemplate then give to others all that's granted from above.

You, St. Dominic, saw your children under Mary's mantle blest.
Pray that, once our life is over, we may know eternal rest;
And with all the Order's saints, our service finished, we will be
Happy to be counted as a part of your great family.

In Honor of St. Catherine

Dominic's daughter, Siena's patron,
Blessed Catherine, hear us raise
Voices now in joyful anthem
As we celebrate your praise.
You have given faithful witness
To God's truth and strength and light
As you strove with valiant courage
To defend each human right.

Serving God as papal counsel
And the friend of sick and poor,
Advocate for social justice,
Writer, guide, and so much more.
As His bride the Lord has chosen
You to walk His mystic way;
Thus we honor saint and Doctor,
Seer and Sister on this day.

Dear St. Catherine, be our model;
Be our inspiration, too;
Help renew our firm commitment
To God's will in all we do,
Till we follow your example,
And with all the saints above
 We rejoice in blissful glory,
Aflame in His eternal love.

A Blessing

Because I know God's mercy,
　　have felt His gentle touch
Upon my broken heartstrings
　　as He plucks notes to soar
Above life's fragile failings,
　　through grief—and more,
Beyond dark, desperate moments
　　when self seems all too much;

Because God loves me to healing acceptance
,　　caressing my soul to song,
　Together now we hymn the strain
　　that lilts above shadowed gloom and pain
And warmly enfolds all the world in
　　merciful blessing.

We Are. . .

Earthenware jars of mystery:
Ill-formed or graceful,
All bear the same inscrutable
Treasure: spark of Divinity.
God's Spirit lives in us.

Discounting outer forms:
Whether battered, bruised, broken—
No matter the size, shape, hue, pattern,
We value most reverently
Treasure borne inside.

I bow in awe at the beautiful, ineffable
Mystery you carry within.
The God within me
Recognizes the God in you.

Honora's Prayer

I've known joyous decades—vibrant, hope-filled, yet earth-bound—
Marvelous, magical moments and memories.
Solitary silence envelopes me now, cocooning cares
And concerns, while God prepares my soul for transformation.

Lately, lofty visions have faded, blurred; senses dulled;
Within there grows a certitude:
I am destined for cataclysmic   upheaval.
No, rather: **radiant revelation**:
Exhilarating change, renewal of life.

I know it near, tantalizingly close:
I feel it on the tip of my heart.
Yes! God shatters my chrysalis;
He allows me to test my tremulous, fragile wings

Until at last I fly free—
Free to Eternity!

A Choice

Those who love are wondrous wise,
Knowing full well the price
For opening hearts, sharing lives
May often cut like knife-thrusts,
May sometimes sear like flame.

Yet choosing NOT to love
Beats a ponderous drum-roll
Signaling melancholy marches
Toward lonely life and desolate death.

Better far to suffer scars and scorch
Than exist unknown, unloved, unmourned.

You're It!

Whee! Look at me:
I'm a big red balloon
Blown near bursting
with breath of the Spirit.
She leads me to flee
Earth's drear bounds and fly—
A daring, dancing dot
chasing errant clouds
And playing tag
with butterflies.
I toss you a kiss
and skim above
Tree tops.
(Pity them, stodgily rooted.)
Now I swoop down
and tag <u>you.</u>
Come,
join me
as we soar
aloft—
Happy,
joyous,
and free!

Jessie

Jessie doesn't like me. I know it.
Her nose wrinkles like an old prune
When she sees me coming,
And her eyes crinkle into dark slits
Like hard sticks. Jessie's mouth
Pinches into a small **o** at me
Instead of the dimpled smiles
She gives to Billy—and Tommy—
And prac'ly all the boys.
Her chin lifts to point at the sky
 When she sees me.
Jessie doesn't like me.
 So how can I love her,
As the Bible tells me to?

Shadows on the Moon

A full moon torments me with its borrowed beams;
Long, silvery fingers stretch across black velvet sky,
Freezing my heart with icicle touch,
  Leering, sneering, jeering at my loss.

  (Where is the kindly moon of lovers, dreamers?
  What perversity permits a miscreant to linger
    with viciously chilling power?)

Hurry, friendly cloud-puffs, cover it now;
Banish this mocking, merciless villain;
Toss obscuring shadows on
That taunting, haunting face.

Change

Bare brown branches blotch the snowy landscape;
Twisted tree tops feather-dust a pale gray day;
A few brave birds barter songs for grain.
"Winter's back is broken," wise folks say.
In these bleak days of weakened winter
A weary, wizened ancient tyrant-king
Sulkily cedes his icy throne to
Bright-eyed, sprightly Spring.
And I—how long will it be till I,
Weary unto death with sorrow's clammy chill,
Heed Spirit's challenge, and change
My stubborn mind, frozen heart, obdurate will?

Memento

I treasure
even faded memories of you,
Tenderly unfolding
as buds open their hearts.

(Recalling intimate moments,
Softly sorting through silken petals.)

Do you, Sweet Love,
Do you remember, too?

Trinity

Here in our midst
Churns enough power
To change the world,
For the Father is here—

Impregnable.

Here in our midst
Yearns enough hope
To anchor the world,
For the Son is here—

Invincible.

Here in our midst
Burns enough love
To inflame the world,
For the Spirit is here—

Unquenchable.

Woman Anointed?

Because I am a woman, my lips may not express
Words of consecration; my hands may never bless,
Or grant forgiveness. Liturgical, high praise
Is not mine to offer. Subservient, silent: the way
I'm bid to serve my Church because I am a woman.

BUT—

Because I am a woman, my heart feels
   boundless love.
My dedicated spirit soars high and far above.
Compassionately purposed, Baptismal
   anointing sure,
Hands, heart, and spirit know sacral mission pure.

Because I am a woman!

Morning

Dearly do I love the sun that brings me
A giant cup of joy as I begin my prayers.
Then God, sun, and I
Form a Trinity of Light
Bright enough, strong enough
To meet life's challenges
One day at a time.

Margie's Lament

(A true incident: she watched the helicopter take her husband to the hospital after a massive heart attack)

He flew away while I stood watching
Red lights shrink smaller, fainter
In darkest pre-dawn.
Climbing, the plane flew beyond my sight,
Above my farthest reach.

Oh, could he not know I stood alone
And tarry just a while?
Could he not say, "Go back—go back
To where my love waits,
And let me have but one more moment"?
No; not one moment—never again a moment,
Never again a shared kiss.

"And then he died," the doctor said.
"And then he died?" I asked—
"And then he died?" in frantic disbelief,
Until the truth could no longer be denied.

In spirit swoop back down to me, my Eagle;
Visit me again with your dear strength.
Whistle your tunes, smile your tenderness,
Ease my aching heart with your pure love.

"I Have Called You by Name"

God rakes the raw edges of my soul,
Dredging the ragged depths, uprooting
Intricate, enigmatic, mysteriously dark
Shrouds—stripping away a lifetime's
Morass of tangled, knotted gnarlings.

Only His love-sharpened vision
Could spy a gleam, a faint glimmer
Of God-life flickering through
Twisted, murky underbrush.

Only Love's keen eyes detect
A hint, dimly tenebrous,
Of almost imperceptible promise.

Then—"Thea," He calls me. "Thea.   My Own."
And, reborn, I am named.

Part II: Introduction

A while ago, someone asked me:
"What is God like?"

I started thinking about that question;
I haven't stopped yet.

God-life is all around me:
in Nature, in everyday events
and circumstances—
most of all, in people.

"What is God like?"
Like the air, water, fire, earth.
Like everything and everyone alive.

Maybe these few simple pages
will help <u>you,</u> too,
find comparisons.

Life-giving God of strength, your own Son called himself the **"Bread of Life."** You are **bread** to your starving people: life - giving nourishment and sustenance at its most basic. You have been manna in desert wanderings, and you still fill us with all we need whenever we ask. When we turn to you, we approach the table of elemental goodness, of pure and wholesome happiness. You help us survive the famine of faithlessness by feeding our hungry souls with your Godliness. I lovingly accept you, my God; I desire with all my being to "taste and see" your sweetness. **Fill me with yourself,** loving and compassionate God, and I shall indeed be satisfied.

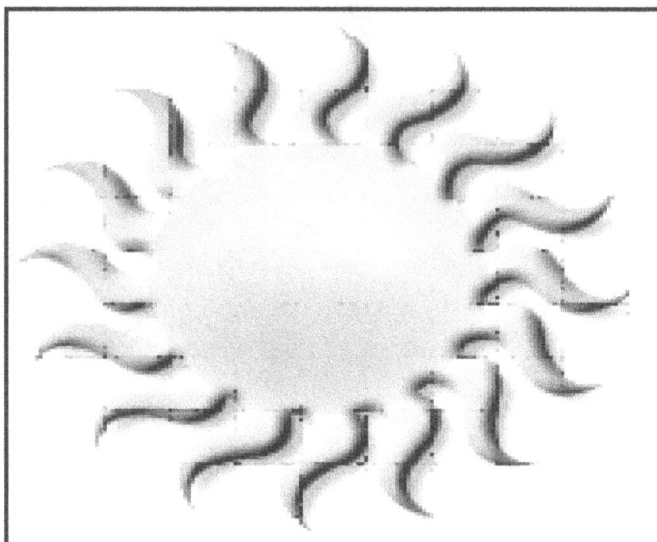

Sun-God, **God of fire and passion**, you are the source of all life, all energy. Your luminous glory demands a shield for our weak vision: we cannot bear to gaze on your brilliant, celestial radiance. From you shine the grace-giving promises of growth, warmth, and fiery redemption—proof of your glowing, ardent love for all your creatures. Without you we are nothing but ice-locked inertia, frozen inactivity. Warm us to life, flaming God; call us to growth in your love. Renew us in our Baptismal promises to follow your loving and certain paths for our lives. Strengthen in us the faith that the Blessed Trinity is ever in-dwelling in our souls, guiding us to transformation. Inflame us to re dedicate ourselves passionately to your service, God of ardor, **God of love**, that we may spend our lives spreading the love you have shown for us and all your children.

Masterful **Artist- God,** you have breathed all living things into being through the sharing of your loving creativity. Everything in the universe is an expression of your goodness, reflecting your artistry in myriad ways. God of color, line, and form, you grace the world with your beauty, and we rejoice in your life - giving inspirations. Above and through all, you constantly manifest respect for materials you use to fashion your splendid masterpieces, especially the greatest one of all: the souls made in your own image, my Beloved **Artist-God**

Human friendship learns from you, my faithful **God, my Friend**, infinitely more beloved than any earthly one. I love you. You have plumbed the depths of my being; you know all my secret desires, frailties, and failures. Yet you love me. I place my trust and confidence in you, for I know you will never abandon me, never forsake me. My heart leaps in joyous amazement that you should care for me as you do; it is a tribute to your goodness, for I do not deserve a friend like you. When I fail in following you as I should, like a good friend you show me the right path; gently but firmly you lead me in the way of Truth and Justice. You teach me the way I should treat others when I see how you treat me and other sinners like me. In union with you I find my peace and happiness, **Beloved Friend, Beloved God.**

Ever-present God, I see you in the faces of those whom I encounter daily, in both formal and informal occasions. Please compensate them for mistakes I have made in our relationships. Bless all your children; gladden their hearts with the certainty of your love; enlighten their paths. Have mercy on us, all-caring God, and reward those who have humbly ministered to me while I, in proud self-sufficiency, thought I was ministering to them. I beg your compassionate tenderness for every one of us, most loving and gracious God. You know the pitfalls and troubles that may befall us; grant us your compassionate love and grace to conquer temptations and to lead a fruitful and holy life, **ever in union with You**.

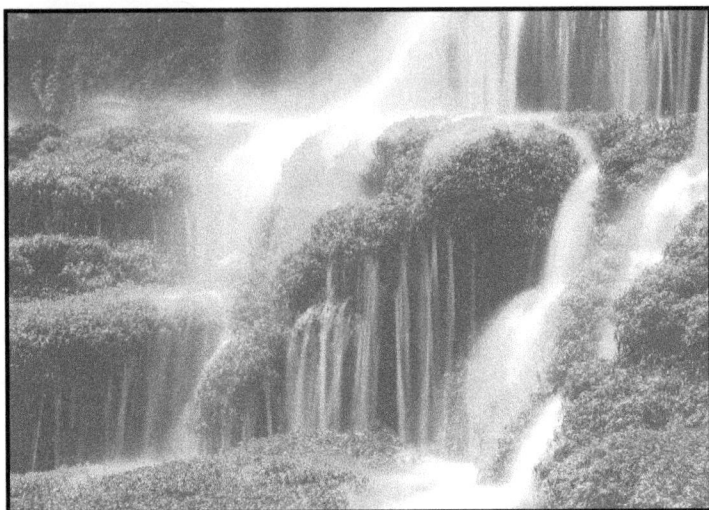

My God, you are like a breath-taking, powerful waterfall. The tremendous cascade of your powerful love energizes me; the majesty of your life-giving flood rejuvenates my weakness, restoring and renewing even as it cleanses. You purify my intentions; you purge my soul of selfishness; I am lost in the rushing waters of your love, which sweeps away all dross in its might. Take me, my God; use me for your purposes; unite my shallow stream to your roaring avalanche of love, power, and energy. Let me be lost in you, God, my powerful waterfall. Then I shall know what you are and what I am; only then will I experience true and lasting love in your **compassionate, great, and merciful heart, which yearns for our love**.

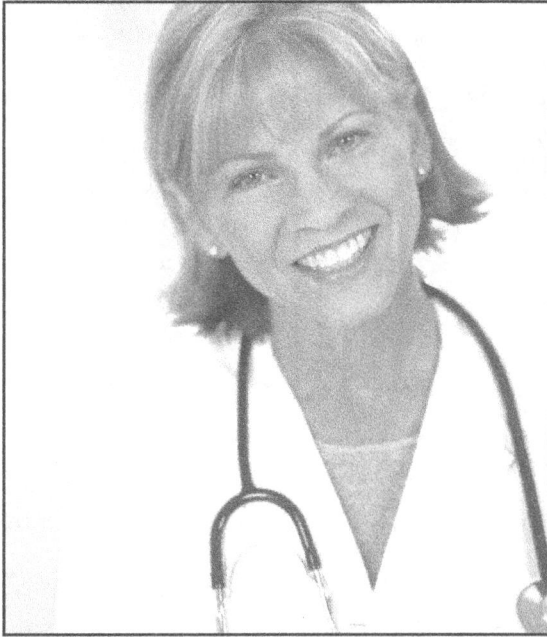

Merciful God, you are like a kind, intelligent, perceptive, generous, most gentle physician. We come to you in pain and misery; you diagnose the illness, prescribe the remedy, and monitor our halting progress toward renewed spiritual health. Your great love guarantees our full and complete recovery, if only we listen to you. Your prescriptions may at times seem bitter or unpalatable; but, trusting in your care, we follow your advice, which always insures a life of peace, justice, and love. Your loving concern and patience with us can never be fully recognized by our fragile, selfish hearts, but we are grateful for the all-encompassing love which prompts them. We are unworthy of your never-failing love for us. Thank you for making house calls to my weak and needy soul, **loving and divine Physician.**

You are like lilting music, rhapsodic melody, and toe-tapping movement, **God of dance, harmony, and rhythm.** How my heart sings to you, how my spirit dances with joy! You bring a delicate balance and equilibrium to my life; you pluck upon my soul-strings and fill my being with love-songs of magical charm and cadence. You thrill me with rapture; you stir me with your lyric love. Lead, and I shall follow, for I realize that you know the way to Perfect Happiness. Continue to enthrall me with your magic, choreographing and enticing me into your exquisite and stirring **Dance of Love, my God!**

Living and gracious God, you are like a rainbow. You brighten our days with the promise of your unceasing care for us, your everlasting love and merciful forgiveness. You paint our skies with colors of encouragement and hope; you bring beauty, peace, and happiness to our lives time and time again. When I am downcast or discouraged, the remembrance of your constant rainbow love brings me joy and courage. My heart sings and my soul expands with grateful love for you. You are all I long for at rainbow's end. Teach me and help me to bring rainbow love to others who need assurance of your care and concern. Burst forth in me, my God, that I may bear witness **to your Rainbow Love.**

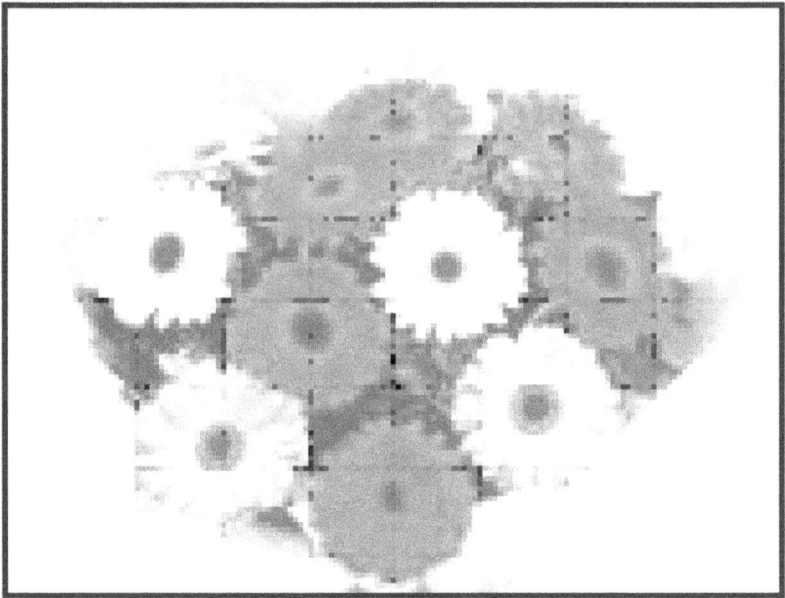

God of all Beauty, you are like a world of flowers. Your devoted actions in our lives are like sweet, fragrant blossoms, both a gracious reward and a delightful surprise to those who love you. With color and texture you beautify our lives, offering hope and happiness to bless and brighten our days. Help us to cultivate the soil of our hearts, preparing them for the mystery of your growth in us—your presence in every aspect of life. Come, live in me, God of all that is good and holy. Bloom abundantly in my heart; fill me with yourself, **God of loveliness!**

Beloved Mother-God, lovingly pregnant with each of us until the time of our birth in Christ-life, you carry within you the seed of our true selves. Nurturing, sustaining, feeding us with your own substance, you offer us an unselfish haven, support, and unconditional love. With amiability and compassion you listen to our cries, gently hushing our fears, tenderly heeding and granting our mewling requests. Embrace us still and always, patient, loving, and generous Mother; bring us safely Home to you, exquisitely **sensitive and loving Mother-God**

Father-God, my soul rests in you. In you I find all-encompassing, unconditional love. You offer my heart a serene haven, a safe shelter from the storms which trouble me and often lead me astray. You gently guide me, pointing out the way to happiness. In the security of your forgiving love, my soul is at home, at peace. Keep me ever close to you, Abba; protect me from myself and my weaknesses. In reverencing your name and recognizing your fatherly care for me, I find true and lasting joy. You are my strength, hope, and comfort, **my Father-God, my Love.**

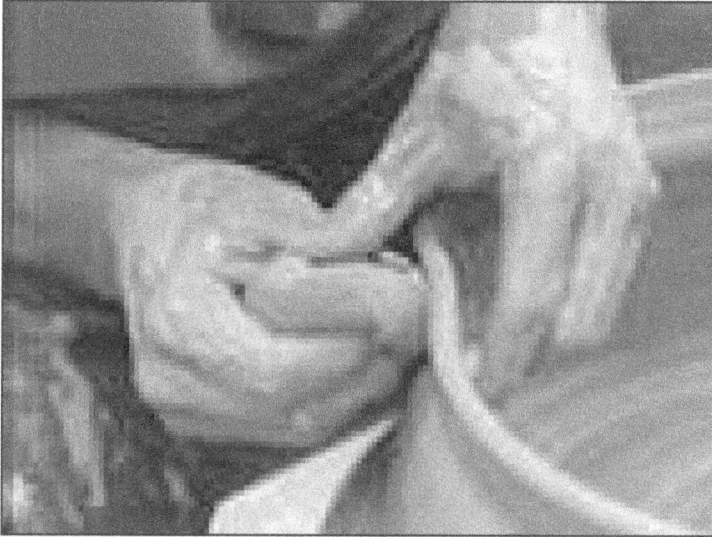

You are like a potter, Creator-God. Upon the creative wheel of your Divine Providence you throw the humble clay of my being. You shape with your strong, energizing hands; you fashion me according to your will. Sometimes I stubbornly resist your artistry. But your loving patience far exceeds my stubbornness and pride. Again and again you mold me, never allowing me to thwart your loving, wise designs. I am grateful for your masterly touch, great Artist of my soul. Form me as you will; I abandon myself to you. Take me, use me, make of me a work of art, **Beloved Potter-God.**

You are like a lover, God of my heart. Take me; I am yours. Gentle me in the stillness of your spirit; quiet me in the hidden recesses of my soul. Enfold me in your loving embrace; I long to be entirely and completely yours. Subdue every single thing in me that is not of you, for you. Whatever you deign to do to me, I accept; I truly abandon myself to doing only your holy will. If ever I should stubbornly resist, then be **not** gentle, my only Beloved. Seduce me, ravish me, conquer me by any means that will really unite us. I yearn to be lost in you, so that your love inundates my soul, carrying away myself and leaving only you, **God my Lover.**

My God, you are like a **lovely butterfly,** bringing joyful delight to my soul when I remember your graceful dance to win me. You woo me with your soaring glides as you lead me high above crass, worldly concerns. You prove your ardor in countless, persistent swoops down to me, offering grace—mine, just for the taking. You have earned my love through your goodness; you have captured my heart with your eternal beauty. I long to share your flight of freedom, happiness, and hope. Being lifted above all mundane cares, I want to live in love with you, **God, my beautiful One.**

All-knowing God, you are like a whole library, a marvelous compendium of eternal knowledge and righteousness. In you rest all the answers, all the guidance I shall ever need or want. Yours is the beauty, the order of law and certainty; philosophers, scientists, wise men and women throughout the centuries have tried in vain to plumb at least a modicum of your knowledge, for in you reside the fullness of wisdom and understanding. I humbly bow before your omniscience. You formed us before the ages began; you sustain us by your goodness and love. You are Truth and Justice and every virtue; everything good is only a faint reflection of you. **I praise you and love you, my one true God.**

Afterthought

*Of course we all realize that God can be
neither named nor defined.*

*The best we can do is to find some
poor basis of comparison.*

*I realize I have taken liberties
with images of our all-powerful,
mighty Creator.*

*Perhaps someday you and I
will find other answers
to the question
"What is God like?"*

Part III: Introduction:

Rockin' Chair Reflections

Sit back, relax, and spend a few minutes thinking about something besides money worries, pet peeves, annoyances, football, American Idol, the weather, evening news, or TV soaps.

Here are a few topics to help you get started.

A Special Ministry

(Racine Dominican Sisters were once asked to respond to a questionnaire : "How do you see your ministry as part of our Dominican charism?" This was my response.)

Head bowed, eyes downcast, he sat there with the towel draped around his sagging shoulders. Just for a flashing instant I saw not the frail invalid, but Jesus mocked by the soldiers in Pilate's courtyard. My heart swelled with compassionate love for him and for the Christ in him, and I remembered Jesus' statement to Catherine of Siena: *"I have placed you in the midst of your brethren that you may do for them what you are unable to do for me."* That is the motivation for my care of Father Barron.

Rev. William Robert Barron, O. P. preached the Day of Recollection prior to my entrance into the Racine Dominican Postulate in February 1943. Our next encounter occurred in Santa Fe, New Mexico; he was a Professor of Theology at the then St. Michaels's College; he was also the confessor ministering to our Sisters at Our Lady of Guadalupe Convent. Our relationship blossomed from teacher-student, confessor-penitent to friend-friend.

Father suffered a major stroke in 1974, and was subsequently sent to eight different nursing homes. He did not do well in any of them. "There is no such thing as a good nursing home," he said; "there are just some not as bad as the others."

In September 1982, Father Barron was moved to Kundig Center in Detroit; I assured Father Ebben, Provincial of the Southern

Province, that I would look after Father Bob and do my best to see he would not feel as lonely, depressed, and abandoned as he had felt in the past. But he suffered <u>another</u> stroke in October—one that left him yet more debilitated with aspirated pneumonia, since he was unable to swallow food.

He underwent surgery to insert a gastrostomy tube, and was eventually released from the hospital in December—released to **my** care because Kundig Center was not equipped to handle medical patients. "Just make him comfortable," the doctor said; "he will not last until Christmas." Rather than send Father to another nursing home, I asked permission of his superiors and mine to care for him in my apartment.

He was completely dependent on me at first: I changed his diapers, bathed and shaved him, administered tube-feedings after liquefying a variety of nutritious foods. He slept twenty-two hours a day, totally disinterested in his surroundings—depressed, dejected, frustrated. He had forgotten how to read or tell time; watching television was no joy: all he saw was a meaningless blur of color and disjointed movements.

"I'm not good for anything," he moaned. "Just let me die: throw me out with the garbage!" I tried reasoning with him, reminding him about having faith in God's Providence. "Are YOU preaching to me?" he demanded. **"I am the theologian!"**

Then I tried a new strategy, framing whatever idea I wanted to communicate to him as: "Twenty years ago you taught us that..."

That worked fine, and soon he was remembering that it was through His redemptive suffering that Jesus is Savior; he joined his own sufferings to that of Christ, taking upon himself the mission to pray for the world. That intention gave his life meaning and purpose, and he soon began to recover.

"He will not last until Christmas," the doctor had said. But he didn't say **which** Christmas, and as I thanked God for Bob's renewed life, I also prayed for patience in caring for him.

Father Bob learned his numbers through a simple card game I devised primarily to entice him to leave his bed; he read newspaper headlines to me as I cleaned the room; he answered my numerous questions about football and baseball games on TV; from the bed, he instructed me in the techniques of golf. We prayed together, using the familiar old formulas as well as spontaneous outpourings. He was, however, unable to express himself coherently, so I attempted to read his mind and heart and give utterance to whatever I sensed he was thinking and feeling. It was often amazing to both of us how God allowed that to happen.

The pastor of the parish to which I belonged resisted adding Father Bob's name to the list of those to whom Holy Communion would be administered monthly. He thought Bob was not sufficiently aware to receive the Host. But I knew that my friend had been unduly upset and agitated at the pastor's visit, sensing the negative, judgmental attitude of the older man and reacting accordingly.

I asked another priest to meet and evaluate Bob; he did, and soon he was returning regularly to administer the sacrament. Later I was given permission to have Consecrated Hosts in a little "chapel" in our home; every morning I lit candles and together we sang the " Adoro Te" and "O Sacrum Convivium" "just as the other Dominicans do," he said.   It made him happy to be assured he was still a member of the Order, still joining in the work for God and His people.

And so life continued for twelve years—Not easy for me, certainly a great suffering for Father Bob. Seeing this once vibrant, active, extremely gifted and intelligent priest reduced to a helpless shadow of his former self—totally dependent on others—has given me lessons in a humility I had never envisioned. Realizing my awe-ful responsibilities in caring for him has made me weigh my words, monitor my too-quick reactions, and emphasize praise and encouragement not only to him, but to my associates, students, and all whom I contact.

For in this ailing priest I saw all of humanity. We each bear a cross; all of us share in the suffering of Christ in one way or another; we experience, to a greater or lesser degree, the same insecurities, doubts, depressions. We all wait for the shining glorious moment of Paschal Victory, for if we have suffered with Him, we will surely conquer with Him. Caring for Father Barron has opened my eyes to the suffering Christ all around me; it has expanded my horizons, enlarged my heart, and deepened my compassion. This special ministry has given me a deeper sense of the beauty of the human soul, a certainty of each individual's need for love, acceptance, and appreciation.

How do I see this as part of my Dominican charism, you ask. There was need, and I was able to answer it. I thank God for this beautiful and rewarding part of my life.

Acceptance of Suffering

We accept this mystery with love and faith: we who follow Christ will suffer. We probably will not be nailed to a cross, however. Ours will be little splinters from the cross: others' actions, the loss of loved ones, the loss of part of ourselves as we bear the gradual weakening accompanying advancing years. These do not mirror the agonies of war, violence, bloodshed—but they are enough to remind us that ours is a life of suffering.

Saints Cornelius and Cyprian, whose names we mention in the Canon of every Mass--accepted and even embraced the suffering that Divine Providence permitted in their lives. The first part of the epistle we heard today seems to foretell the kinds of difficulties to be encountered by both Pope Cornelius, Bishop of Rome; and Cyprian, Bishop of Carthage. Both saints, truly pastoral, guided the Church through difficult times, comforting and encouraging their people and each other when unbelievers persecuted and eventually beheaded them within five years of each other in the third century.

In the second part of the epistle, Paul reminds us of the source of our hope, the reason why we do not despair. Every time we drink of the Eucharistic cup, he writes, we proclaim the death of the Lord. That means we also proclaim His resurrection. Through patient suffering and death, we attain eternal life with God. The Pascal Mystery speaks strongly to those who will listen, as Cornelius and Cyprian did in their day, as you and I strive to do daily.

Individuals like you and me, as well as other members of religious or civic communities, citizens of different countries, members of the Church, inhabitants of the whole earth—saints and sinners, we all suffer. This past year has been traumatic for all of us on many different levels. What do we do with the pain? How do we deal with it?

The centurion mentioned in today's gospel gives us an example. "I am not worthy," he said. In other words, "I am broken, fragmented, vulnerable; I need healing." When we admit that to God, to ourselves, and to others--when we acknowledge our weakness and imperfection, we prepare ourselves to receive God's choicest favors. One of those blessings is the serene acceptance of suffering, which permits God to work in us and through us.

In the dark moments of suffering, God is tenderly parting the fibers of our being, penetrating to the very marrow of our substance, preparing us for union with Christ. In this and every liturgy, we are given the opportunity to begin this union. As a loving bride we receive the sacramental Body of Christ, Who gathers all of us—His Mystical Body--to Himself in merciful blessing. We say in humble sincerity, "I am not worthy." And He compassionately accepts and sanctifies our unworthiness, gradually and gently transforming it into strength. In this way we are enabled to live for God and for each other as we journey together toward Eternity. This is the blessed hope we find amidst our suffering.

Faith

Both readings today deal with FAITH. In the first, God sends word to Ahaz that he should remain tranquil and not fear his enemies, that God Himself would save the people. The Gospel reiterates this theme of faith—or lack of it.

But I'm sure that everyone here is faith-filled. When we are asked to declare our belief in God during the Mass, I answer with a firm "I do believe," and I hear strong voices around me affirming the same thing. Faith is alive and well here, isn't it? **Isn't it?**

Faith is certainly an outstanding characteristic of our heritage, from Dominic on down through the centuries. Remember how firmly the early Dominicans believed? When terrorists invaded the monastery and stormed into the chapel where the friars were praying Compline, those men continued to sing the <u>Salve</u> even as the barbarians murdered their brothers one by one. We commemorate their courage and faith by singing the <u>Salve</u> at the death of every Dominican.

Yes, we do believe the principal doctrines of the Church, and perhaps we would even die for our Faith. But what about some of the more gentle parts of Scripture? When God tells us through the prophets that we are loved with an everlasting love, that we are the apple of His eye, that God finds joy in us, do we really believe it-- even when we are discouraged or downcast as we read newspaper accounts about those suffering in our world?

I know that during the times when I am sick and tired of being sick and tired, it takes strong faith truly to believe that God is always with us, loving us, consoling us as a mother would. Have you experienced the same thing when you are ill, worried or concerned? We don't always FEEL that consolation: sometimes our energy is depleted and we are emotionally numb, but we still BELIEVE in God's loving care, don't we?

Jesus said, "As the Father has loved me, so do I love you. Abide in my love." Do we? Do we believe Isaiah when he tells us that even though a woman should forget the child of her womb, yet God will not forget us; that He knows us so well and loves us so dearly that we are carved on the palm of His hand. Jesus compared Himself to a mother-hen, longing to gather her young under her wings. Do we believe that God loves us that way, that She is concerned about us, that She laughs with us, weeps with us; that God cares for all Her suffering children more than we do?

Or are we like the apostles, to whom Jesus said, "Oh foolish ones, why did you doubt?" Is our faith really as strong as it could be, or must you—like me--say to God, "I believe. Lord, help my unbelief"?

Lemon Drops and Love

Elongated, flickering shadows chased each other across the wall, and I hesitated a bit before entering her darkened room. *"Dzien dobrie, Nenna,"* I whispered, the Polish greeting stumbling awkwardly from my four-year-old lips.   Nenna, my great-grandmother, sat up a little in her bed and motioned me nearer.

Vigil lights before her statue of the Sacred Heart burned more brightly, it seemed, as she smiled and held out her arms. I crept closer, and we gazed at each other—the frail octogenarian and the chubby child— unable to communicate verbally, but comfortable, nonetheless.

As usual, she had a bag of hard candy at hand. Offering a piece to me, she smiled again, her wrinkled face beaming with love; I felt her cold, thin fingers and smelled her lemony breath. *"Ja chen kocham, Nenna,"* I said, bashfully trying out another Polish phrase. "Ah, Florenz," she murmured, and hugged me as her stream of unfamiliar words washed over me: their meaning unclear, but Nenna's obvious sentiments warming my heart, making me feel safe and loved.

I remembered that scene several months later as I stood transfixed alongside Nenna's new narrow bed, moved now to the living room. Nenna lay on a satin pillow, but she wasn't smiling, and she did not have her bag of lemon drops. The Sacred Heart statue was there, and vigil lights burned, but the room wasn't dark—it was light; and people sat on chairs placed around the room. Everything was different, and I felt confused. Nenna never once opened her eyes, even when I reached out to touch her.

"No, Honey," my mother said. "Don't touch."

I looked up at her, puzzled and bewildered. "Why not? Nenna always likes...."

But Mom shook her head, and I noticed that her eyes, wet and shiny, leaked a few tears down her face.

"What's the matter? What's wrong? I—" But I was told to "Shush," and I knew what **that** meant. So I stood quietly next to Mom when she sat down with the other grown-ups.

Then Auntie Gustie came in and said in a soft voice that dinner was ready, and we could come in now. I understood, and it sounded normal, although I wondered if there would be enough for so many people—some of whom I didn't even recognize. They got up and started going to the dining room; one of the ladies took Mom by the arm and walked in with her as they whispered some things to each other. I stayed behind, waiting for the old people to leave.

When the glass doors between the living-and dining-rooms were closed and I was alone, I felt more at ease. "This is my chance to talk to Nenna," I thought; I went over to her long, strange-looking bed and bent down to whisper my recently-memorized phrases to her. She still wouldn't open her eyes, so I touched her hands which were crossed over her chest, an old brown rosary entwined between her fingers. I had often seen it just that way, but never before had Nenna been so still, so silent; and her hands had never felt this cold and stiff.

"This isn't Nenna," I thought. "Someone is trying to fool us by putting a big doll in her place!" I opened my mouth to protest the cruel hoax, but just then my mother entered, looking for me.

"Florence," she said sternly, "what are you doing here?"

When I explained that I only wanted to talk to Nenna and get a hug and a lemon drop, Mom pulled me to her and explained that my great-grandmother had gone to Heaven, to be with God forever. I didn't understand how Nenna could be in Heaven and still be **here**, too; Mom said that we'd talk about that later.

One thing bothered me, though. "Will God let her keep her lemon drops?" I asked.

"God loves Nenna, even more than you do," my mother answered. "He will let her have whatever she wants."

"Goody!" I said. "And when I see her again, maybe she'll give me one, if I can still remember some Polish."

"Whether you remember the Polish or not, Nenna will give you all the lemon drops you want," my mother assured me. "She loves you very much; you are special to her because you are her first great-grandchild."

For three-quarters of a century I have cherished those memories; with joyful expectation I think Heaven will be all the sweeter because of Nenna's lemon drops and love.

Loneliness

"I'm lonely," the eighty-eight-year-old Sister said. "I've never been so lonesome in my life." I was able to resonate with her feelings because intuition tells me that many other elderly people would admit the same. Could it be, however, that this emotion is not the negative thing we usually consider it, but instead an expected—even welcome—sign of maturity? growth?

Of course, we affirm and rejoice in our social nature. We are divinely destined to reach our full potential in relationship both to God and to each other. Even recent brain-wave experiments have demonstrated that we are "wired for prayer" and for human interaction. But as we advance in years, experiencing the disappointment, disillusionment, and ultimate failure of our various addictions, we are forced to realize that we are vulnerable, flawed, imperfect beings. We are empty; we have nothing in and of ourselves. We are an aching void, waiting to be filled. We are lonely. Lonely for God.

When Jesus said "Blessed are the poor in spirit," perhaps He referred to those who sink to their knees in humble acknowledgement of their abjection, wailing aloud to God in helpless abandonment and surrender. "Lord, to whom shall we go?" Peter asked many years ago. We powerless ones ask the same question today: to whom shall we go except to the One Who has extravagantly showered us with unconditional, unchanging love throughout our lives?

Centuries ago, when St. Augustine proclaimed "Thou hast made us for Thyself, O Lord, and our hearts are restless until they rest in Thee," he was speaking from a heart wounded by misplaced, misdirected—and ultimately unsatisfying--love. Wordsworth echoed these sentiments when he admitted, "We have squandered our hearts away." Haven't we all looked back with rueful regret and confessed, "Too late have I known Thee, too late have I loved Thee, Oh Beauty ever ancient and ever new" ? What are these expressions but admissions of a soul-deep loneliness, an existential longing for union with the One Who Alone can fill our emptiness?

This soul-hunger becomes more apparent as we suffer losses consequent upon the aging process. All that we clutched in foolish possessiveness has gradually been taken from us: our prestige, status, authority, competency—and more discernible faculties like mobility, sight, hearing, memory. We feel diminished. But under all the losses, like the serene depths of an ocean even when a storm is raging, there   lies the certainty of a value far surpassing what we have lost.   Dawning upon our consciousness is the understanding that we <u>must </u>be emptied of all that is not divine so that God can fill us completely.

Ours is a holy and wholesome loneliness. . .loneliness waiting for companionship, union, fulfillment.   In our loneliest hours, the spark of God-life ignited in our souls at Baptism flares out
in yearning desire to be utterly consumed by the Flame of Love Whom we call God.

St.Augustine's Feast,

August 28

As Paul notes in his Letter to the Thessalonians, he drew courage from God to preach the Gospel in the midst of much struggle. Augustine, whose feast we celebrate, could have said the same. We, having grappled with our own difficulties, can sympathize with at least some of both Paul's and Augustine's inner conflicts: —temporary espousal of various heresies and early leanings toward licentiousness, as well as arrogance and pride. But above and through all, their noble hearts ever yearned for some- thing MORE—always MORE than any earthly, intellectual, or physical pleasure could bring.

Haven't we experienced that inner longing and wondered what it meant? One day my teacher quoted Augustine : "Thou has made us for Thyself, O Lord; and our hearts are restless until they rest in Thee." I immediately resonated with that quote, and felt intense joy knowing that Augustine could help me resolve the restless dissatisfaction and disillusionment with current teenage concerns. Later, when I studied literary criticism, I was assigned the reading of Augustine's Confessions—not because of its theo-centrism, not because of his desire to experience God even in this life—but because of his innovative teachings about the human condition—what touches the human heart and motivates the will—statements rich in psychological insight as yet unknown to scholars of Augustine's time. He is recognized as the first psychologist— a compassionate, understanding one--and I joined classmates in praising his humanistic perceptions. His comments laid the foundation for our Catholic social principles, the basis of the Church's concern for peace and justice.

At the close of his letter, Paul writes that he has been gentle with the early Christians, holding them in such great affection that he shared with them not only the Gospel, but his very self as well. Isn't that exactly what Augustine did? He has shared with us his interior struggles, sins, successes and failures—"Warts and all," as we say. One particular incident has impressed me. When his mother, St. Monica, died, Augustine, the revered Bishop of Hippo, wept openly and sobbed in sorrow. One well-meaning member of his ecclesiastical household reproved him for his tears, offering a pious comment about God's Will. Augustine paused a moment, then replied, "Brother, not for an instant would I want to subvert God's Will for my darling mother. But I am human, and I must express my grief."

Perhaps that is the reason for his prodigious renown, even more than the hundreds of books attributed to him: he trusted us enough to let us see his weaknesses. Isn't that true in our own lives, too? When anyone trusts us enough to share frailties, mistakes, woundedness, our hearts open to that person.

The Gospel warns us against hypocrisy. Augustine, too, repudiated that vice. He advocated that Christians be not concerned about others' judgments, caring only that God is with us, reading our hearts, discerning our inner intentions. "Love, and do what you will," Augustine once said, knowing that if we truly love, we will do only what pleases the Beloved. And no matter how difficult the task is, he said, "Where there is love, there is no labor; or if there be labor, the labor itself is love." The quote I love best, especially now, at this time of my life, is: "Late have I known thee; late have I loved Thee, O Beauty ever ancient and ever new." Augustine said **late**. He did not say **too late** because he knew that it is never too late to change, to grow, to love.

Since Dominic chose the flexible Rule of St. Augustine for his own Order and because Thomas Aquinas was influenced more by Augustine than by Aristotle, Augustine has been called the "Grandfather of Dominicans." On his feastday we can be justifiably proud of our illustrious grandfather. And, if we take time to meditate on some of his words, our Grandpa Gus will be proud of us!

Consecrated Life

As we are reminded every time we receive Holy Communion we are all ONE in Christ. Through His incarnation, the greatest event in human history, **all** our lives are consecrated.

I learned about consecrated lives by observing my mother and father. Through sixty-two years of joyful love, despite sickness and setbacks, poverty and pain, they lived their faith, were true to each other and to their children. Many—though not all--have similar histories to share.

But a loving Divine Providence cares for those whose family-lives were less than ideal. We have known other good people who have sacrificed homes, families of their own while caring for ailing parents, or by living as good Christians among their friends and neighbors. These lives are consecrated, too, because of their love.

On all sides we hear that modern youth searches for community. **All** of us reach out, search, yearn for something that takes us out of ourselves to connect with something greater, more noble than our fractured, fragile selves and limited powers permit.

Long ago, my mother told me lovers learn that more important than either I or you is **WE**. I did not understand it at the time, but now I do. In religious community, we experience the awesome blessing and responsibility called interdependence. We entrust to each other our goods, our liberties, our lives. There is a reason we are called **Sisters**.

As Sisters, we stand on the shoulders of 800 years of earlier Dominicans, in more than 100 countries. Future generations, we trust, will live and preach the ideals, charisms, prophetic stance of the Order in ways we cannot even dream of. Today, we are privileged to belong to an interdependent community, accomplishing something far greater together than any thing any one of us could achieve alone.

When Vilhaljamur Stefansson and his associate explorers and scientists needed volunteers to the South Pole almost a hundred years ago, Stefansson advertised for men courageous enough to endure bone-chilling cold, difficult menial work, loneliness, danger, isolation, unknown perils. "How will you ever attract workers with an ad like that?" some asked.

But engineers, teachers, men with successful careers answered in amazing numbers for lowly jobs with no pay, incredibly attracted by such statements as :"The attainment of the purposes of this expedition is more important than the safe bringing-back of the ship...even the lives of the party are secondary to the accomplishment of the work."

This is what it means to be taken up out of yourself, willing to suffer for the sake of some lofty, splendid enterprise....even earthly scientific knowledge. Isn't there something in your heart that stirs at such stories? That wants to imitate such nobility?

Chardin wrote : "The day will come when, after harnessing space, the winds, the tides and gravitation, we shall harness for God the energies of love. And on that day, for the second time in the history of the world, we shall have discovered fire. "

Then we will all be LIVING our vocation as consecrated people. As people called to greatness, we will repudiate the false values of the world. With eyes opened by the Holy Spirit, we will recognize greed, violence, and the lust for power or possessions as the evil that they are—and then deny them any place in our lives.

It all comes together, doesn't it? We are a consecrated people, called by God to serve others. It is a matter of record, one government official told me, that more Christians than anyone else follow the service avocations generous workers of all kinds--whose goal is to serve others, no matter what the cost.

Could that be because we hear the poignant cry of God, "Whom shall I send?" and in consecrated love and generosity, we answer: "Here I am. Send me. **USE me.**"

Holy Thursday: Thoughts Remembered from Prayer Services

The Triduum: The Triduum is really ONE celebration, from Holy Thursday until the end of Holy Saturday's liturgy. There is no dismissal from Thursday's Mass: no "Go, the Mass is ended"; there is neither greeting at nor dismissal from Friday's services; only when the Holy Saturday's liturgy has been ended is there the glorious "Ite—Alleluia!" All ONE celebration—the institution of the Eucharist, Christ's suffering and death, His resurrection: all ONE: the Paschal mystery.

Holy Thursday and the Washing of the Feet: If you draw a stick figure of a man standing upright, what do you have to do to the drawing in order to show him washing someone's feet? You have to bend the line, show the man bent over, kneeling, humbling himself, ready to serve. It is fitting that the Triduum begins this way, opening the Paschal Mystery with the astounding sight of the God-man stooping to serve His Own creatures, to wash their feet.

Feet: Every one of us has some mark of beauty about us: some have brilliant eyes, or a smiling mouth; hair—or the lack thereof—but very few of us display our feet. In fact, millions of dollars are spent hiding and protecting our feet, washing, massaging, powdering them so they won't smell....We pretty much keep our feet to ourselves. It is no wonder that Peter pulled away, probably stuck his feet under his robes when Jesus bent to wash them. They were dirty from trekking through the dirt and sand; maybe the toenails were black and misshapen; they smelled from the work and travels of the day...Peter was ashamed of himself and his poor smelly old feet.

And we—don't we act the same when we are conscious of our weakness, our vulnerability? It's easy to go to God when we are a success, when we are satisfied with ourselves, when the world looks bright and rosy. But when we stink with the sweat of our humanity, when the world—our frailties—have dirtied us, we hide in confusion and unfounded fear. Like Peter, however, we eventually realize that those are the times when we most need the healing, cleansing touch of Christ; we cry out with Peter, "Wash me wholly, Lord!"

Kneeling before the Cross: A beggar kneels when requesting favors; a slave kneels before his master; a lover kneels before the beloved; a creature kneels before her God; a prisoner kneels as he asks pardon; a humbled and contrite person has been "brought to his knees".....all of these are appropriate postures, and all of them describe our relationship with our God. It is right and fitting that as we are shown the instrument of our salvation, the Cross, we should kneel....

Smell the perfume of the oils: Let its sweetness delight you, and know that God is your ultimate Delight; rub it into your skin; savor it; carry its fragrance with you....

Prelude to Holy Thursday

The musical "Jesus Christ, Superstar" shows us a tormented Jesus in the Garden of Gethsemane, weeping and crying out to God in agony. We addicts have known similar agony. We hold it in our hands now, mystically joining it to the suffering of Christ. During this liturgical celebration, we expose our communal woundedness to the merciful compassion of our God. We ask God to look upon our frailty, to accept our brokenness and sanctify it as Jesus' suffering was sanctified—for the salvation of all humanity.

In this commemoration of the Last Supper, we unite with Christ and His priests down through the ages as we joyfully, gratefully acknowledge our share in that priesthood. With unconditional love and deep humility, we have "priested" each other. Not with sacred oils have we been anointed, but with the sanctified and sanctifying tears of our Sisters. Wounded healers guided by the Spirit, we have ministered to each other in ways beyond the world's fathoming. And, with hearts brimming with love and gratitude, we now—as a community--praise God for blessing us, entrusting us, with pain—allowing us to share in our own humanness the price of His vulnerability.

Holy Thursday Experience

It's been many months since the experience, yet the memory is still fresh, slipping quietly between the concerns of ordinary life like a sweet, familiar melody drifting through my day, bringing me comfort.

It was Holy Thursday. I had volunteered to be one of the participants in the washing-of-the-feet ceremony. At the proper time, therefore, I walked up the few altar steps, sat on the bench, and waited.

Father Paul Colloton, OP, was the presider that evening. Paul and I have been friends for more than a decade, but neither one of us had ever had occasion to talk about our feet, so I presumed he would be unpleasantly surprised when he saw them for the first time. They are not pretty. I have had five separate surgeries on my feet, along with fractured bones and misshapen, arthritic toes. As I removed my shoes, I smiled at Paul in rueful regret, in embarrassed apology.

But I was the one to be surprised—and stirred. Kneeling before me, Paul took my foot in his hands and did more than wash it: he caressed, anointed, and blessed it.. I watched, breathless, as he touched my deformed foot with such tenderness that I felt a lump form in my throat. As his hand lightly glided over a particularly red, swollen part, he looked up at me, his eyes asking, "Does that hurt?" My slight nod called forth still more gentleness; his sensitivity and compassion touched my heart as he lovingly cared for my right foot.

Then he repeated the warm and careful kindness with the left one. As Paul ministered to me, in imagination I saw Christ kneeling there in his place. It was Christ Who touched me in such loving kindheartedness; it was He Who washed, anointed, blessed—not just my feet, but my heart and spirit---healing old hurts, disappointments, regrets. . . .

Eyes filled with tears of gratitude and awe, I rose from the stool with difficulty, helped by Christ/Paul, and returned to my former place.

The inexpressible, haunting memory of that experience has elevated my spirit and filled it with grateful song. I hope I will remember it as long as I live: the time I felt that Christ had really, physically touched me.

Feast of St. Peter of Verona

This Gospel message is certainly not new. Nobody reaches the age of ten without experiencing suffering. And now, as many of us are approaching or already in our twilight years, we live intimately with pain and diminishment of all kinds. But Jesus tells us that suffering is only a prelude to what is yet to come. We are an Easter people—a Paschal people—and our faith assures us that we are to go courageously through the Passion with Christ before joining Him in glory.

If only we could keep that thought in mind when we are actually in pain—whether physical, mental, or emotional....It's not easy then, is it? But those are the times when community helps us. There is always some one who—by word or example--reminds us of our destiny and gets us back on track again.

Today we share another blessing of community: we celebrate the feastday of our brother, Peter of Verona, gaining incentive and inspiration from him. When Peter was 15 years old, he heard St. Dominic preach and was so inspired that he petitioned for reception into the Order, receiving the habit from the beloved founder himself. Peter became renowned as a powerful preacher—so strong, in fact, that he offended some hardened sinners. One of those who objected to Peter's unwavering preaching of the truth was Caroli, a violent man who attacked the preacher with a large knife.

I have recently examined a holy card which shows the courageous priest holding a palm signifying martyrdom, with a knife cutting his skull and another one piercing his chest. Big drops of bright red blood stain his white scapular. According to witnesses, Peter fell to the ground, dipped a finger in his own blood, and wrote CREDO—I believe. With his last breath, Peter forgave his murderer. Caroli repented, then eventually entered the Order, hoping to take Peter's place.

How was Peter able to perform such a heroic act of faith and forgiveness? I suggest the answer lies in the magnificent feast we have been celebrating all week: the presence of the Holy Spirit in our lives. As we were so beautifully reminded by our anointing last Sunday, we were gifted with the Holy Spirit through our Baptism and strengthened by Confirmation. When we were confirmed, the Bishop gave us a slight blow on our cheeks to remind us that we were to be brave soldiers of Jesus Christ, as Paul enjoins us in today's epistle.

Credo in unum Deum

We have certainly been hearing much about soldiers lately, haven't we? Tens of thousands of valiant, courageous ones like Pat Tillman and Joe Durban or our brothers, uncles, cousins, nephews, honored just last Monday; others, not so admirable—and we know which ones we would like to imitate.

Then, even though we may have to endure chains—and chains come in all kinds, sorts, and varieties--we will remember that the Word of God will _never_ be chained; and if we allow the Spirit free and full access to our lives, we may become worthy sisters of Dominic, Catherine, Benedicta, and Peter the Martyr.

Bread of Life

Less than four months ago we gathered in this chapel to celebrate Christmas, and we rejoiced that Divinity had come to us as Emmanuel, "God With Us." The chapel was ablaze with lights and color, with banners and poinsettias; we were jubilant— rightly so. Today we again meet in a chapel decorated with fragrant flowers, seeing banners adorned with butterflies—symbol of new life—to remind us that we are an Easter people, and our song is "Allelluia!" We meditate during this Paschal season on a great mystery. Not only did Christ give Himself to us as **brother** at Bethlehem; not only did He give Himself to us as **Savior** on Calvary; now He gives Himself to us as **food** at our altar. In today's Gospel He calls Himself "the Living Bread."

Bread—most common, most ordinary—found in every country, in every culture, eaten in banquet halls of the wealthy, in hovels of the poor; relished by the strong and weak, by young and old. Remember the comforting milk-toast your mother used to prepare for you when you were ill? Some day—unable to manage other dishes--we will be glad for a piece of bread soaked in weak tea.

Why did Jesus choose such a lowly food, so commonplace, so familiar? We take it for granted, as we do water—or even breathing. But its very ordinariness tells us something: just as we need bread to sustain physical life, we need Jesus, the living bread, for a healthy soul-life. When we receive Him in the Eucharist, we become one with Him and we affirm our union with Him and with all others who receive.

In the early ages of the Church, the Eucharistic minister said to each communicant, "Receive the Body of Christ," and the answer was given: "I do" or "I will," as couples respond when the priest asks them about their commitment to each other in Matrimony. Ever since I learned that, I have been so glad that the soul never ages, because I try to approach my reception of the Eucharist not as a tired old woman, but as an eager bride, full of ardor, aflame with love. Yes, I do receive the Body of Christ; yes, I do give myself to my Beloved, and I do accept Him whole-heartedly. _Yes. Amen_.

But this is not a passive reception—something done while we are half-asleep or distracted; we dynamically will that He receive us and lead us to the Father and the Holy Spirit; we joyously become one with the Divine, lovingly surrendering ourselves to God's work in us. We resolve to be Living Bread as He is. How can we do that? How can we be bread to each other?

In accepting the Eucharist, we accept the WHOLE CHRIST— including the anguished people of the world who starve for God's healing touch—for Christ Himself. Certainly we include in our prayerful concern the suffering ones in the Middle East, in Latin America, in our own country's squalid inner cities. None are excluded from our compassionate love. But here in our midst, people around us are hungry, too—hungry for our acceptance, our affection, our attention. Our own Sisters and the others with whom we come in contact long for a smile, a friendly word, some notice that they are alive, that they count. They, too, need the living bread of our kindness, our engagement, our love.

Jesus says, "I have loved you to my death. I have worn myself out for you. Just as you eat bread and drink wine, you have eaten Me up, too. Now I want you to give yourself to others as completely as I have given Myself to you." St. Augustine said that in the Eucharist we receive What we are: the Body of Christ. As the Body of Christ, we are *eucharist*—beautiful gift-- to each other. "I am the Bread of Life," Jesus said. He invites us to be the same.

Feast of the Immaculate Conception:
December 8

I'll call her Rita. Before I met her, she had already ministered as a medical missionary in Africa for more than 20 years. Rita had great stories to share—instances of faith, courage—and other stories unutterably tragic. One of the latter involved two girls—ages 14 and 15—who had been raped by soldiers a few weeks previously. They came to Rita in great agony, begging her to abort their babies. They knew that if the villagers discovered the pregnancies, the girls—and possibly their entire families could be killed—or at least banished, all their belongings burned.

More than two thousand years earlier, another young girl knew of **her** village's customs regarding unwed mothers: the scorn, contempt, mockery—often being stoning to death—they and their families faced. She knew, this Mary of Nazareth—and when God's messenger proposed to her the plan of the Almighty One, she was frightened—who wouldn't be? But, since courage is fear that has said its prayers, and her love was far greater than fear could ever be, she said YES.

How was she able to do this, to give her whole-hearted "Be it done to me"? With Karl Rahner and Denis Edwards we believe that "all human beings always and everywhere exist as surrounded, shaped, and constituted by the presence of God's grace." Does that explain it? Others have not responded so generously, but then no others have ever been called **"Full** of grace."

In the climax of the play "Waiting" set in the Ante-room of Heaven, Eve tells the women of the Old Testament about God's plan for humanity's redemption: the Messiah will be born of a woman. "Of a **woman**?!" the others cry. "How can that be? In our world women are considered weak, inferior, worthless...." But Eve reminds them: "The world has seen through YOU that women can be as loving as Sarah, as brave as Judith, as loyal as Ruth, as wise as Deborah...This Mary, chosen by the Father, espoused to the Spirit and incarnating the Son, possesses all these virtues..."

Father Charles McCarthy says that it is through Mary that we learn of God and God's ways. She shows us the **human side of God's perfections**. And it is now, today, here, that we **imitate Mary imitating God**. We counteract the violence of the world through our nurturing love; we renounce the selfishness of a hedonistic life-style by our chastity; we repudiate materialism and consumerism by our life of simplicity; we reject the mad pursuit of power by obedience to God, no matter what is asked of us.

Mary is human like us, but sinless like the Son she bore. All humanity has been consecrated by Jesus and Mary. Together they have birthed us to a new life as members of the Mystical Body—a life we renew each time we receive the Eucharist.

Recognizing Jesus--1

Jesus joined the disciples on their way to Emmaus, but **something prevented them from recognizing Him,** just as something occasionally prevents us from recognizing Him today.

I recently heard about Betty, who was driving her expensive automobile through a deserted street when she felt, heard, and saw a big rock impacting the vehicle. Startled, she glanced out of the rear-view window, furious when she saw a small boy still holding other rocks, obviously intending to throw them, too. Betty quickly parked her dented car and shouted at the boy. "You young rascal, what do you think you're doing?"

I'm sorry, Miss," the boy stammered, "I had to get somebody's attention. I need help for my brother." Then Betty saw why the lad's brother needed help. A hefty teen-ager was lying near the curb, an over-turned wheelchair on top of him. The younger brother was too small to up-end the wheelchair; he had resorted to throwing rocks to attract attention.

Betty helped the boys, then walked back to her car. *My life is like that,* she thought. *Sometimes I don't hear the voice of God; I have to have rocks thrown at me before I get the message.* Unlike Betty, I haven't had any rocks thrown at me yet, but God has used other means to get me to pay attention to Him. Just like the disciples on the road to Emmaus, I, too, have experienced barriers to prevent the recognition of Christ in my life. Sometimes, when my pride or selfishness blinds me, I become oblivious to others' goodness or needs. Then I erect figurative walls behind which I hide my guilt or seek comfort from foolish actions. Such barriers prevent me from seeing Jesus in those around me, and I persist in my self-destructive activities, not really aware of my neighbors' hurts or needs, just speeding, racing along, doing my own thing.

But what really matters is not what we're **doing;** it's what we are **becoming** that's important as we journey together. Are we becoming more aware of the God Who accompanies us? Do we hear His quiet invitations, His callings to our spirits? Can we discern the divine spark within our companions, or are we blinded by self-absorption, surrounded by walls of our own making? Are we so oblivious to the call of God and others that we need a rock to capture our attention?

God calls to us in our prayer, through circumstances and events, through our companions. Repeatedly we are urged to seek and find Him. Clutching our old attitudes and habits, we can resist change—or we can accept it and thereby grow in love and understanding. We can open our eyes to the inspirational reality around us; we can see Jesus as He is in Himself and as He reveals Himself in the love, compassion, and wisdom of others. We can heed God's call for help to the needy and marginalized in society—even the forgotten, neglected, lonely ones sitting next to us.

Listening, we gradually abandon our old selves and false comforts, and are re-born to new acceptance and appreciation of life. Then, in the "breaking of the bread," as we receive what we proclaim to believe, the Body of Christ lives in us, and we know Him and each other as part of Him.

Recognizing Jesus--2

I don't know what prevented the disciples from recognizing Jesus—but I am aware of some of the barriers which prevent me from recognizing Him in my life. Perhaps some of you can identify with them. We, too, are on a journey—though a much longer one than the trip from Jerusalem to Emmaus. We all grope through the labyrinthine darkness of our brokenness, discouragement, and pain, stumbling toward the Light. Occasionally I am blinded by expectations—my own expectations about myself or others—and what I perceive as others' expectations about me.

Then I lose focus and become lost, unable to find God. But in His mercy He comes to me, just as Christ appeared to the disciples on the road to Emmaus, and tells me that what really matters is not what I'm doing; it's what I am becoming as I journey. Am I becoming more aware of the God Who accompanies me in the everyday persons, places, events, and circumstances of my life? Do I hear His quiet invitations, His soft whisperings to my spirit? Regrettably, I often concentrate on THINGS—or on ideas and concepts, just as the disciples did. They asked the stranger, "Haven't you heard about the things that have been happening?" Then they admitted, "We had expected that..."

But no one can build a relationship with concepts, things, or expectations. We build relationships with people—with a person, like Jesus. When we heed the gentle intervention of Jesus in our lives we begin to understand Who He is and who we are. And it is only when we know ourselves, our weaknesses and strengths, that we can begin to know the compassionate Christ.

Those disciples on the road to Emmaus were humble enough to accept the mild reproof of the Stranger: "O foolish and slow of heart," He chided them. But they were docile—willing to be taught—and they opened their minds and hearts to Him. Once they established that relationship with Jesus—the relationship which He Himself had initiated--they couldn't get enough. "Oh, stay with us," they begged.

Haven't we, too, experienced how, when we admit our vulnerability, when we acknowledge our great need, our hearts burn within us at Christ's words, at His unconditional love for us? As we listen to His voice and surrender our lives to Him, we gradually abandon our old selves and false comforts and are re-born to a new awareness and appreciation of God's presence in us and among us.

Then we open our hearts and receive the Beloved One in Whom we have placed our faith and hope. After experiencing that great Eucharist, we are able to experience eucharist with a small e and recognize that we are *beautiful gift* to each other. With great joy we go forth to minister to others, proclaiming that Jesus lives—that He is indeed alive —and that we know Him in "the breaking of the bread."

Recognizing Jesus--3

Jesus joined the disciples on their way to Emmaus, but **something prevented them from recognizing Him. . .** just as something occasionally prevents us from recognizing Him today. Intellectually we acknowledge that Baptism makes us one in the Lord; we joyfully embrace our brotherhood. But there is something other than intellect operative in our lives; we are defined not merely by rationality, but also by emotions. It is those emotions that often pose stumbling blocks to our full acceptance of the truth.

Frequently, when our bias or prejudice results in cruel words or actions, we erect walls to hide our guilt or engage in other defensive tactics. Such defenses prevent us from seeing Jesus, and we foolishly seek ease in performing a multitude of tasks, keeping busy just for the sake of busy-ness.

What matters is not what we're **doing;** it's what we are **becoming** that's important as we journey together. Are we becoming more aware of the God Who accompanies us? Can we discern the divine spark within our companions, or are we blinded by self-absorption, surrounded by walls of our own making?

Literature abounds with unknown and unrecognized loves: fairy tales like "Beauty and the Beast," classics like <u>Sense and Sensibility</u> or <u>Our Mutual Friend</u>, modern films like "Lost in Translation" symbolize universal truths. Clutching our pre-conceived notions, we can resist change—or we can accept it and thereby grow in understanding. We can open our eyes to the inspirational reality around us; we can see Jesus as He is in Himself and as He reveals Himself in the love, compassion, and wisdom of our companions.

Then, in the "breaking of the bread," as we receive What we proclaim to believe, the Body of Christ lives on in us, and we accept each other as part of Him.

Service to Others

As a child, I was enthralled with fairy tales, delighting in stories of maidens in distress saved by courageous knights. I thrilled to the love which overcame all obstacles, and felt deep satisfaction at "happily-ever-after" endings. I remember asking my mother, "What did Dad do to make you fall in love with him?" then being disappointed when she spoke about kindness and generosity and good humor. I persisted: "What **great things did he do** to win your love?"   My childish mind could not understand a love prompted by such ordinary things--not nearly as romantic as slaying dragons, climbing snow-capped mountains, or swimming across mighty seas.

But now I recognize the quiet nobility of those qualities which Paul talks about in today's epistle: compassion, kindness, humility, gentleness, forgiveness, gratitude, love. These simple virtues are made manifest in the lives of the good people around us. We practice them too, don't we?   Margaret of Hungary did. She was a princess who lived in mid-13th century—born to the King and Queen of Hungary. Her parents had vowed to consecrate their child to God if their country would be liberated from their enemies; their four-year-old daughter was, therefore, invested with the Dominican habit.

Despite having her life planned by her parents, she was happy, spending her days in contemplation and penance. When she was 18, her father wanted her to marry the King of Bohemia, but Margaret refused.   All accounts of her life call attention to her spirit of renunciation and humility, as she discharged the most menial tasks in the community.   She was prayerful, loving.   But Margaret performed no miracles, founded no monasteries, converted no heretics. She did the simple, ordinary, everyday duties of her state in life—and when her life ended at the age of 29, she was regarded as a saint.

Seven hundred years later, during World War II, many churches were destroyed, including one in England—where, remarkably—a statue of Christ was left standing.   Unfortunately, however, the statue's hands had been blown away.   The pastor, instead of lamenting over what had been taken away, rejoiced in what was left. He painted a sign and placed it at the base of the statue: *Christ has no hands but yours.*

Imitating Margaret, we remember that today: Christ has no hands but ours to wheel a chair down the corridor, to bring someone a glass of water or a cup of tea; He has no lips but ours to smile, to offer a word of congratulation or sympathy, affirmation or support; no ears but ours to listen to a story, to hear someone's troubles; no heart but ours to offer compassionate love and understanding.

In today's Gospel, Jesus tells us, "Unless the grain of wheat falls to the ground and dies, it remains just a grain of wheat; but if it dies, it produces much fruit. Whoever loves her life loses it, and whoever hates her life in this world will preserve it for eternal life." That's what Margaret of Hungary did; that's what we are called to do: die to self, be content, even **joyful,** to surrender all we are and have, so that God takes over more and more of our being, and the Divine Light shines in us and through us to others. Christ has no hands but ours: may we use them lovingly for others as He did, as Margaret of Hungary did.

Suffering

There's no escaping it—we are going to suffer. One way or another, every one of us will suffer physically, mentally or psychologically-- perhaps **all** those ways. And no one can really tell us **why.** Oh they can say it's because God loves us and wants to purify us; He doesn't cause suffering—He merely allows it. But we believe in a God of mercy, compassion and unconditional love. Does a loving mother, father, or friend let a loved one suffer, when he or she could prevent it?

Many years ago I attended summer school with a woman who asked me those questions. I spent time with her, expounding what I had heard about how God doesn't directly **will** suffering, but only **permits** it. She thanked me as we parted, and said: " I understand everything you said, and I agree. But—" she asked piteously, "**why** does God permit suffering?"

I didn't know then, and I don't know now. What I do know today is that none of us will ever fully understand the Mind of God, and that it is the most egregious kind of pride to assume that anyone ever could. The Hindu mystic Sri Ramakrishna has offered us good advice: "Resign everything to God. Surrender yourself. . . then there will be no more confusion." And St. Theresa of Avila wrote: "The soul must forget about understanding and abandon itself into the arms of Love."

God asks us to accept this mystery with love and faith: we who follow the Man of Sorrows will suffer. No, we probably won't be crowned with thorns, scourged, and crucified. Ours will be little splinters from the cross: someone's irritating manners, another's unkind misinterpretation or insensitive remark; the loss of loved ones, the loss of part of <u>ourselves</u> as we bear the headaches and arthritis, the forgetfulness and stumbling of our advancing years. These may not be world-shattering incidents of tragedy; they may not mirror the agony of victims of war, violence, blood-shed—but they are enough to remind us that ours is a life of suffering.

Saints Cyril and Methodius, whose feast we celebrate today, accepted and even embraced the suffering that Providence permitted in their lives. Sons of wealthy Greek parents, these brothers were so skilled in linguistics that they were able to bring the Cyrillic alphabet to the Slavs, Poles, and Russians, translating Greek and Latin into the language of the people. Constantine—he wasn't called Cyril until shortly before his death—and his older brother Methodius courageously braved the opposition of the ecclesiastical authorities of their day, and enabled the people to read Scriptures and celebrate Mass in their own language.

Cyril was the studious one, and died an early death after enduring slander and calumny, misunderstanding and vituperation. Methodius was the dynamo, the go-getter. He became a bishop—but even then, when he persisted in his efforts to use the vernacular instead of Latin in worship, he was cruelly criticized—even imprisoned—by fellow clerics.

Suffering is part of our vocation as Christians. But what will we do with the pain? How will we deal with it? Recently I heard about a young woman who complained about her painful burdens. Her mother took her into the kitchen where she filled three pots with water. In the first, she placed a carrot; in the second, an egg; and in the last, she put some ground coffee beans. After about twenty minutes, the older woman turned off the boiling water. She fished the carrot out and placed it in a bowl. She did the same with the egg. Then she poured the coffee into a cup. Turning to her daughter, she asked, "Which are you?

"When adversity comes into your life, how do you deal with it? Are you like the carrot, which seems strong, but when troubles come, it wilts, becomes soft, and loses its strength? Or are you like the egg, which starts with a strong outer shell protecting its fluid interior, a tender heart, but after a trial becomes stiff, resistant, hard-boiled? Or are you like the coffee bean? The bean actually changes the hot water, the very circumstance that brings pain. When the water gets hot, the coffee bean releases its fragrance and flavor."

How will **we** handle the suffering which comes into our lives? Will we imitate Jesus and the saints in their loving acceptance of God's Providence? Will we be carrot, egg, or coffee bean?

January 1: Feast of Mary, Mother of God

"Hail Mary, Mother of God…" How easily the words flow from our hearts and lips! And rightly so — the celebration of Mary as Mother of God is the oldest of all Marian celebrations, dating back at least to the third century. But in the fifth century great controversy arose, with some arguing that Mary was indeed the Mother of Christ, but to call her Mother of God was going too far.

The Council of Ephesus in 431 resolved the matter for believers, affirming that Mary is truly the Mother of God. The council's documents were in Greek, and the term used for Mary was "Theotokos," God-bearer. We take nothing away from Mary when we recognize that we, to, are God-bearers, carrying the Divine Spark enkindled in us at Baptism, nurtured by the Spirit, and flaming up throughout our lives in ardent desire to be united to its Source. Mary was the first; she is our model; we are her grateful and loving children. And as her children, we look for the family resemblance.

Our lives may not parallel her life in superficialities, but they do match hers on a deeper level. In order to find a sure way to union with her Son, w can examine Mary's responses to God's invitations to her, and imitate her, our model, our mother.

From earliest womanhood, Mary was asked to make drastic changes in her life: from maiden to mother, from the familiar to the foreign, from the joyful lullabies of Bethlehem to the raucous soldiers' jeers at Calvary, from relative obscurity to notoriety and public pain. Gospel accounts, as recorded in Luke's Infancy Narrative, with which we have been filling our hearts these past weeks, offer many examples of farewell and turning, of a variety of changes. Most of the scenes end in departure:

- After Mary *visits* Elizabeth, she *returned* to her home;
- Mary and Joseph *change* their abode and *travel* to Bethlehem;
- The shepherds *go* to Bethlehem, but then *return* to the fields;
- Mary and Joseph *leave* Bethlehem, *travel* to Egypt, then *leave* that place and *move* to Nazareth.

In every departure we leave something behind and move toward something new. But we need not fear. Whatever the future holds, whatever problems, adversities, or sufferings lie ahead, we take courage and strength from our Mother's example. God travels with us since we, like Mary, bear Him within us. And like Mary, we face the uncertainties with loving trust, with faith and confidence in the Divine Providence which rules our days.

Today we say farewell to the old year and welcome the new. January is named for a Greek mythological figure, Janus, who had one head, but two faces: one to look behind, the other to look forward. On New Year's Day we do that, don't we: consider what the past has been, resolve to make some changes in the future. On the average, according to reports, most such resolves last about 15 days--an indication of the flippancy with which we treat proposed changes in our lives. Yet changes are necessary if we are to grow.

What changes do we truly desire to make—serious, meaningful, quality-of-life changes? What do I want to be different? Is it my negativism, my anger, my warped self-esteem, my illusory expectations of myself and others? If we are not willing to change now, then when? How much time are you sure of?

Now, for the first time this year, we prepare to bring ourselves with our strengths and weaknesses, our gifts and vulnerabilities to the Eucharistic Table, where we will receive What we already are: the Body of Christ. By our "Amen" we signify our belief in that mystery. We receive the sacramental Christ as Mary received the Blessed Fruit of her womb: with humility, with faith, with love. May we make any changes necessary to carry Him to others as she did.

Serenity in the Midst of Distress

Some time ago I saw something which affected me very deeply: a young man walked down the center aisle on his way to receive Communion, his infant son held against his shoulder. The child was asleep, peaceful in his father's arms.

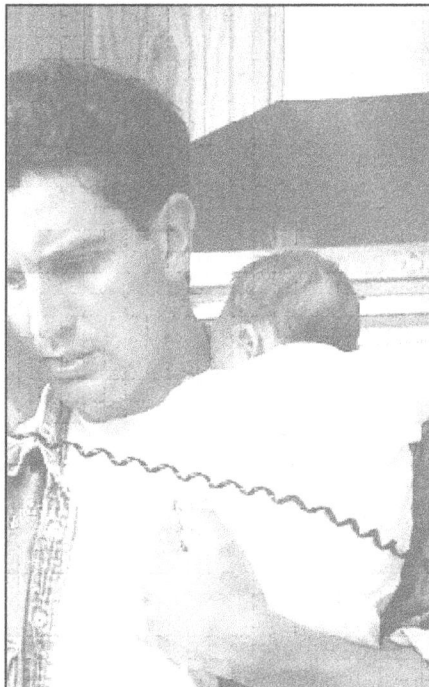

Maybe that kind of serenity is what both Jesus and Paul speak about in today's readings: Jesus tells us that ours is a life of suffering if we follow Him; Paul tells us not to be disturbed by whatever happens, because nothing----
absolutely NOTHING—can separate us from the love o f Christ.

We need those messages, don't we? Every morning's paper, every evening's News reminds us of calamities: explosions, fires, earthquakes, war and its horrible consequences. Any thinking person is tempted to be apprehensive. But today we are reminded that <u>our security is not the absence of danger, but the presence of God.</u> In times of peril God is with us, holding us in love, sharing our heartbreak, sharing our tears.

St. Catherine de Ricci, whose feast we celebrate today, certainly understood that. She, like our other Dominican women saints (Catherine of Siena, who lived 200 years before; Rose of Lima, who lived 100 years after) was a member of the Third Order. Unlike them, however, she did not live at home, but entered a convent. Superiors in the mid-1550's monastery were reluctant to accept her at first because she showed no aptitude for any kind of manual work or for learning to chant the Office. Furthermore, she seemed to be asleep most of the time, unable to join in conversations with other Sisters.

Actually, it was her deeply mystical state and continual interior conversation with God that caused her to suffer many misunderstandings and humiliations. However, she literally allowed nothing to separate her from Christ, maintaining an inner serenity which was a source of edification to others. Eventually her spirituality was recognized: she was chosen prioress, and led her community for more than 40 years with great compassion.

Despite the difficulties she had experienced in her early years, Catherine de Ricci never lost a deep and abiding peace. She realized that peace does not mean to be in a place where there is no noise, trouble, or conflict, but to be in the midst of those things and still be calm in heart...a calmness born of trust in God's Providence. As an experienced sea-farer once said, "I cannot control the winds, but I **can** adjust my sails." We cannot eliminate problems from our lives, but we can adjust our attitudes toward them.

Following Christ, we expect storms; loving Christ, we trust He will carry us through whatever life brings us. We pray: "God, grant me the serenity to accept those things I cannot change; the courage to change those things I can, and wisdom to know the difference." The Source of that wisdom is the Eucharistic Christ, Whom we will soon receive. We prepare to receive, as Catherine did, What we say we are: The Body of Christ. United with His Body throughout the world, through time and eternity, we are One with our Beloved and with each other. And nothing—neither anguish, nor distress, nor peril —will be able to separate us from the love of God in Christ Jesus our Lord.

Relationships

You know, we have advanced admirably in technical matters. We can communicate instantly by phone, fax, e-mail, satellite, iPods, even if it means having my answering service try to contact yours. It seems every time we turn around there's something new on the market—something we ought to have if we want to communicate with each other.

And we have become so efficient: we have identification numbers for Social Security, credit cards, patient or customer services, zip codes, addresses, telephones, drivers' licenses, insurance, and prescriptions. In a recent "House" episode, the forty doctors who applied for positions in his laboratory had to hang **numbers** instead of names to identify themselves.

We are competent about everything except living, about truly relating to each other in an intensely personal, loving way. Why is that? The other night I was watching a television program. A woman, Lynn, was depressed, despondent, considering herself a failure. Lynn couldn't control her four lively, mischievous sons, and she felt she was sadly inferior to her acquaintances, who seemed so perfect, always calm , and"in charge."

Lynn was actually contemplating suicide when two of her friends found her sitting near the lake and approached her, solicitously inquiring what was wrong. When she confided the source of her desperation they assured her she was a good mother, better than they were. "Why, when my daughter was a child," one said, "I wanted to scream with frustration many times!"

The other woman confessed, "I often felt like running away and never coming back — and I had only two children."

"WHY DIDN'T YOU TELL ME ?" Lynn asked. "It would have made me feel so much better to know that I was not a monster-mom, not the only one going through hell with my kids!"

They all laughed after commiserating with each other and exchanging "horror stories" about child - rearing.

But I think Lynn had a good point there. WHY DIDN'T YOU TELL ME? Why WEREN'T YOU WILLING TO SHARE YOUR TROUBLES WITH ME? Why are all of us so ready to tell about our successes, our achievements, our accomplishments, but NOT about our fears, doubts, insecurities?

I don't mean complaining about every little headache, or giving" organ recitals"—intimate details about various surgeries—but interior trials which mark us as vulnerable human being. Of course we would not share such secrets with everyone, all the time—but isn't there something at least vaguely dysfunctional about group of supposed friends if they don't trust ANYBODY, ANYTIME? If after knowing each other for ten, twenty, thirty years, they have to admit, "I really never got to **know** her"? One of the greatest gifts a person can give an other is the disclosure of a weakness, a fault--something that marks him or her as a less- than- perfect human being. Such an admission probably does more than anything else to forge loving relationships; it demonstrates the honesty, trust, and confidence necessary for a true, humble, enduring friendship.

Try it—you'll like it!

Feast of St. Rose of Lima: August 23

Recently a friend of mine visited a relative on his farm. "How's your wheat crop, Uncle Bob?" she asked.

"Well," he drawled, " I didn't plant one."

"Why not?" she exclaimed in surprise. "I thought this was good wheat land."

"I was afeered it would rain," he said.

"Then," she persisted, "what about your corn?"

"Didn't plant none o' that, neither," he said. "I was skeered of corn blight."

"What **did** you plant?" she asked.

"Nothin'. I jest **played it safe**."

Isn't that what we do sometimes? We just **play it safe**, afraid to take a chance, too timid to risk hurt or disappointment by reaching out to others, by doing the noble, generous, **giving deed.** But we are challenged by both liturgical readings and by the celebration of today's feast to rise above such all-too-human inclinations.

Hosea, who was betrayed by an unfaithful wife, compares a sinful Israel to her, and shows us how a compassionate, merciful God reaches out in love and forgiveness, just as the prophet did to his adulterous spouse, just as we must do to anyone who has offended us.

On the eve of His death, the Gospel relates, Jesus told us to love one another as God loves Him and He loves us. **Playing it safe** won't do: we are to love extravagantly, unconditionally, wholeheartedly. And Rose, the first canonized saint and Patroness of the Americas, demonstrates by her life how a woman acts when she refuses to **play it safe** in her love affair with God.

To be honest, for years I mistrusted Rose. Legends about her lying on the ground as a four-year-old and urging her playmates to beat her with sticks so she could feel the pain that Jesus felt during His passion made me wonder if there were some latent masochism lurking in her psyche.

And I, weak and self-indulgent, thought that some of her later penances were extreme, to say the least: winding her long hair around a spike in the wall over her bed so that she would be jolted awake if she fell asleep, exchanging her pillow for a block of wood, hiding a painful crown of thorns under her head-scarf---Such stories "turned me off" and I looked elsewhere for inspiration.

Until I came to realize that "love **does** such things." What lover in history has ever allowed ardor to be circumscribed by rationality, to be framed by what is "feasible" or "sensible" or "practical"? **A lover is an extremist**. Consider how God loves us into being—not because of anything we might be or do, but only because the ineffable Divine Goodness compels Godhead to share Itself.

Remember how Jesus loved us unto death, stretching out His arms on the cross in an embrace wide enough to enfold us all. He didn't **play it safe.**

And consider Rose of Lima—"Rose of St. Mary," as she liked to be called. She, as a Dominican tertiary, acted in direct contradiction to the culture and mores of her time in a life of penance and service to the poor. One room of her tiny house was set up as a place where she could care for the elderly sick—even the pagan Indians. In addition, she endured her own infirmities without question, without complaint. She saw her pain as sacramental, and united it to the sufferings of Jesus for the salvation of the world. **She** didn't **play it safe**.

What comments would she make if she were here today and observed the way I bear my splinters from the Cross— what if **she** waited a bit longer to be served meals, or sat near someone whose voice or mannerisms irked her, or if she were the object of an insensitive remark? How would she handle the infirmities, the aggravations, the multiple opportunities for helping others, the multiple consequences of aging ?

154

In 16th century Peru, Rose risked her comfort, her energies, her life. But think about what she gained! Jesus called her "Rose of My Heart. . . my chosen bride." And she did not **play it safe.**

Spirituality

"The abyss that is my soul invokes unceasingly the abyss that is my God." So wrote Angelus Silesius, a 17th century philosopher and mystic, reminding us that our hunger for God is always about the pursuit of mystery and the finite nature of our words. The time in which Silesius lived was remarkably like our own, caught up in the anguish and bitterness of religious polemics, embroiled in wrenching political struggles and threats of war. And yet—perhaps as a response to the massive confusion and pain-- spirituality blossomed, just as reports indicate it is doing today.

What is this thing called "spirituality"? Ronald Rolheiser, in his book The Holy Longing, offers multiple definitions, but they are all blended in the concept that spirituality is our response to an inner yearning—a hunger for God—"the abyss that is my soul," as Silesius called it. Millions of men and women around the world have found a depth of spirituality in the Twelve Steps, a spiritual program that focuses on relationship with self, with others, and with God. The program's first three steps can be synthesized in six words: I can't; God can; let Him.

A long time ago I heard an aphorism: "I am nothing, I have nothing, I can do nothing"; and I discarded it in scorn because I thought it was both hypocritical and false. Now, along with many others, I am beginning to recognize its absolute and utter truth: we control nothing; we are the designers of not the smallest iota of our lives or anyone else's. For years some of us went on our merry ways as if we were the drivers of the automobiles of our lives, thinking we were behind the wheels, riding where we willed. In reality, we were cowering in the back seat, furtively peeking out the side window, futilely twirling paper plates in our hands. We were—and are—powerless.

But there is One Who is all-powerful, One Who can and will direct our lives—One Who loves us unconditionally, One Who wills nothing but good. Thomas Aquinas wrote that since God is omnipotent, He could prevent all evil; but instead does something even better: brings good out of it. Our part is to accept, as coming from God's Hands, all the people, events, and circumstances of life.

But this is not a passive acceptance. An old saying advises us: "Work as if everything depended on you; pray as if everything depended on God." We change what we can; we accept the rest in trustful serenity. Since God is directing all life, an appropriate response is trusting in Divine Providence.

> My life is but a weaving between my God and me;
> I may not choose the colors; She weaveth steadily.
> Oftimes She weaveth sorrow; and I, in foolish pride,
> Forget: She sees the upper; and I, the underside.

Sometimes, in group therapy with people who have been psychologically traumatized because of rejection or betrayal, counselors have their clients engage in exercises to help develop trust. A sample exercise is to ask one person to stand behind another, ready to catch the first one as he or she falls backward into the partner's arms. Some clients have great difficulty in letting themselves go, allowing themselves to trust that the others will truly be there for them.

But our God has proved through countless centuries that Divine Love is never-failing, as near to us as our heartbeat, as close to us as we are to ourselves. In times of calamity, suffering, and anguish God never deserts us, never abandons us, never leaves us to our nothingness. He is eager to fill us with Himself; all that is asked of us is to trust.

Today again we pledge our heads, our hearts, and our hands to God's work for justice and peace in the world. And we pray most sincerely: let our efforts begin with ourselves.

Death

I have often marveled at the death of martyrs, such as the 10,000 Koreans we remember today. What gave them the faith and courage to face cruel persecution and agonizing death? I have wondered about the tranquil deaths of our Sisters, too. They lift the veil separating this life from Eternity, often smiling serenely. "What makes them like that?" I muse. "How can they face death with such equanimity and peace, even joy?"

Then I remember autumn and the leaves that change from various shades of green to golden yellow hues, radiant reds, russets, brilliant flame-orange. "Where did all that color come from? What makes the leaves change like that?" I used to ask, until I learned that the colors had been there all the time. It was chlorophyll that colored the leaves green; but as the leaves lost precious sunlight and the chlorophyll receded, the other hues became visible to our eyes.

Perhaps the Korean martyrs—and our own Sisters—face their last hours with faith-filled courage and peace because they have been practicing those virtues all along. A joyful acceptance and a loving willingness to see God in all the workings of their lives has helped them to accept death, too—no matter how it comes: quickly, violently—or a long, slow, fading away—whatever God wills.

In our lives we are not likely to be asked to face persecution and martyrdom; we can paraphrase the questions Paul asks in today's scripture reading: "What can separate us from the love of Christ?

Can illness, infirmity, weakness, depression? Will cancer, diabetes, immobility, aching bones and muscles separate us? Can loneliness, rejection, misunderstandings? **NO !**" we answer.

None of those things can separate us from the God Whom we love—the God to Whom we willingly gave ourselves in youthful fervor, when we answered YES before we really understood what would be asked of us. Now, in more difficult times, are we sometimes inclined to take it back?

We **gave ourselves,** didn't we? And God is taking us at our word. We are not **losing** our health, sight, hearing, strength, memory. We have **given it to HIM.** Like the Korean martyrs, like the martyr-saints of all times, all places, even the places we walk every day, we joyfully, exultantly place our fractured, broken bodies and fading faculties on the paten, to be offered—along with Christ's. We jubilantly add our life's blood to the Precious Blood of Christ and offer it to God without regret, without complaint.

We endure the pain of the cross, encouraged by the example of Christ and strengthened by His Eucharistic Body, knowing that a glorious resurrection awaits us.

We are a Paschal people and our song is **Alleluia,** even if we must sing it with trembling lips and croaking voices: **Alleluia!**

Feast of St. Albert the Great

More than seven hundred years ago today, on November 15, 1280, our Brother Albert died as his fellow Dominicans gathered at his bedside and sang the <u>Salve</u>. During his lifetime, he had been called "Albertus Magnus": Albert the Great. He had used the talents—the gifts God had bestowed on him--so well that people recognized in him the Holy Wisdom which is a sign of God's presence.

Albert had labored as a farmer, and he loved the earth and all living things. He rejoiced in cultivating the land, in planting, nurturing, then harvesting crops and flowers. He had a curious, inquisitive mind and could stand transfixed for hours observing flies, insects, vultures, ostriches, wanting to know the **how** and **why** of things.

Albert did not take easily to studying books, however; and when, in prayer, he heard God calling him to enter the Dominican Order, he couldn't help being hesitant and afraid. But he put himself under Mary's care, and entrusted his vocation to her.

During his Novitiate, however, he confided to a friend, he despaired of ever learning the Latin and Greek he was expected to know, and seriously thought of leaving the community. It was then, Albert himself related, that the Blessed Virgin appeared to him and reassured the Novice that she would obtain for him enough intelligence to excel in all his studies. But, she cautioned, to prove that the gift was due to her intercession—with no honor accruing to Albert himself—before he died, these intellectual gifts would be taken away from him.

It all happened as Mary had said. For more than half a century Albert was truly "the Great One": Cardinal, Archbishop, adviser to the Pope, prior and provincial of his Order, scientist, philosopher, translator, preacher, professor, political peacemaker, linguist, scholar, teacher. He was known, honored, and revered far beyond his beloved Cologne, Ratisbon, and Regensburg. While he was a Professor at the University of Paris, he had instructed both St. Thomas Aquinas and St. Bonaventure. Eventually being named President of the University, he was familiar with the teachings of Aristotle and with the advanced sciences of the Arabic world.

He had long attracted the attention of the hierarchy, and finally the pope, despite Albert's objections, appointed him Archbishop of Cologne, which included Regensburg and Ratisbon. But even as "Archbishop Boots"—so called because he would not ride a horse, but walked, as his parishioners did, through the mud—Albert was as much at ease talking to the common laborers—the farmers and fishermen he met—as he was conversing with the philosophers and theologians. In fact, there were those who sensed that he enjoyed and appreciated the common people even more than he did the intellectuals.

In his last years, Albert lost both his memory and his ability to read or write. Contemporary accounts of his life tell that he remained serene and accepting of God's Providence during this traumatic time. He peacefully spent the closing years of his life in the priory chapel or garden, praying the Rosary and singing hymns to the Blessed Mother.

This, too, was an extraordinary gift: the total abandonment to God in humble acceptance of his weakness and vulnerability.

And who is to say which circumstances accomplished more for the Kingdom of God: as **Albert the Great** or as **Albert the Lesser,** unable to function without assistance, hardly able to remember his prayers, but trusting, nevertheless, in God's unconditional love for him and in Mary's maternal care.

Above all, he found himself constantly drawn to the Heart of Christ in the Holy Eucharist; and, as a true Dominican, he desired to share the blessed moment of sacramental union with others. Thus Holy Communion became for him what the name signifies, union with Christ—with the **whole** Christ, Christ in His Mystical Body.

We ask Albert to pray that we experience the same union: with the sacramental Christ and with each other.

Spirituality and Self-love

"The abyss that is my soul invokes unceasingly the abyss that is my God." So wrote Angelus Silesius, a 17th century philosopher and mystic, reminding us that our hunger for God is never-ending, intensely personal, and limned in mystery.

The time in which Silesius lived was remarkably like the present. People of the 17th century, like those in the 21st, experienced the anguish and bitterness of religious controversy, being embroiled in wrenching political struggles and threats of war. And yet—perhaps as a response to the massive confusion and pain--spirituality blossomed, just as reports indicate it is doing today.

What is this thing called "spirituality"? Ronald Rolheiser, in his book The Holy Longing, offers multiple definitions, but they are all blended in the concept that spirituality is our response to an inner yearning—a hunger for God—"the abyss that is my soul," as Silesius called it.

Millions of men and women around the world have found a depth of spirituality in the Twelve Steps, a spiritual program that focuses on relationship with self, with others, and with God. The program's first three steps can be synthesized in six words: I can't; God can; Let Him.

A long time ago I heard an aphorism: "I am nothing, I have nothing, I can do nothing"; and I discarded it in scorn because I thought it was both hypocritical and false. Now, along with many others, I am beginning to recognize its absolute and utter truth: we control nothing; we are the designers of not the smallest iota of our lives or anyone else's. For years some of us went our merry ways as if we were the drivers of the automobiles of our lives, thinking we were behind the wheels, riding where we willed. In reality, we were cowering in the back seat, furtively peeking out the side window, futilely twirling paper plates in our hands. We were—and are—powerless.

But there is One Who is all-powerful, One Who can and will direct our lives—One Who loves us unconditionally, One Who wills nothing but good. Thomas Aquinas wrote that since God is omnipotent, He could prevent all evil, but instead does something even better: brings good out of it. Our part is to accept, as coming from God's Hands, all the people, events, and circumstances of life. But this is not a passive acceptance. An old saying advises us: "Work as if everything depended on you; pray as if everything depended on God." We change what we can; we accept the rest in trustful serenity.

Since God is directing all life, an appropriate response is trusting in Divine Providence.

"My life is but a weaving between my God and me;
I may not choose the colors; She weaveth steadily.
Oftimes She weaveth sorrow; and I, in foolish pride,
Forget: She sees the upper; and I, the underside."

Sometimes, in group therapy with those who have been psychologically traumatized because of rejection or betrayal, counselors have their clients engage in exercises to help develop trust. A sample exercise is to ask one person to stand behind another, ready to catch the first one as he or she falls backward into the partner's arms. Some clients have great difficulty in letting themselves go, in allowing themselves to trust that the others will truly be there for them.

But our God has proved through countless centuries that Divine Love is never-failing, as near to us as our heartbeat, as close to us as we are to ourselves. In times of calamity, suffering, and anguish God never deserts us, never abandons us, never leaves us to our nothingness. He is eager to fill us with Himself; all that is asked of us is to trust.

A serene trust, according to authors from Thomas Aquinas to G. K. Chesterton and C. S. Lewis, to Thomas Merton, Eugene Kennedy, Henri Nouwen and Ronald Rolheiser, is an indisputable sign of true spirituality, which effects a balance in all aspects of our lives: in our duties and relationships with God, with ourselves, and with others.

Certainly this coincides with Jesus' teaching that we must "Love God above all things, and love our neighbor as ourselves." Most people of a religious bent have no difficulty in recognizing their innate connection with God, the Source of all life and love. Most have no problem with recognizing that in loving God come ultimate peace and happiness. Even loving one's neighbor is clearly understood as a requirement for every person desiring to lead a holy life. Although it is often difficult—sometimes seeming well-nigh impossible—to love our neighbor, we nevertheless keep striving for that ideal. Loving oneself, however, is another matter. Yet a correct self-love is a *sine qua non* of a healthy spirituality.

We acknowledge God-life in Nature: "The world is charged with the grandeur of God," we cry out with the Jesuit poet, Gerard Manley Hopkins. With St. Francis we bless the sun, moon, stars, and all living things, seeing them as manifestations of God's creative power and love. We even see the goodness of God in the holy people around us. "Your goodness and patience mirror God's compassion," we write or say to people who have blessed us. We praise God's work in people struggling to overcome weaknesses; we tell people who have overcome difficulties that we "are proud of" them and their accomplishments. Why do we not easily acknowledge the God-life within **ourselves**, shining out from us, radiating throughout the world, illuminating the pathway for ourselves and others? Unless we value ourselves, philosophers and theologians tell us, our love for God and others is not all it could be.

Why do we not truly value ourselves? Is it from guilt over the past? That may be part of the answer. Deep within us lurks the all-too-human yen to be gods ourselves: to be perfect, to control our lives, our destinies—and the lives and destinies of others. "In Adam's fall/ We sinned all," taught the rhyming catechisms of long ago. Certainly we share the original desire to set our own boundaries, to determine for ourselves the principles by which we live, rather than accepting someone else's decrees—even if that Someone Else is our God and Creator. We have all bitten from the metaphorical apple that we hoped would give us "knowledge [mastery] of good and evil."

And when that failed to materialize, we experienced guilt and remorse over our actions. Not only are we not God, we are not even God's obedient creatures—much less, devoted daughters and sons. We have sinned. God forgives us, but we struggle to forgive ourselves because we are reminded time and time again that we are but human—weak, frail, vulnerable.

In failing to accept ourselves as we truly are, we are burdened with guilt, which inexplicably makes us withdraw from the loving God Who knows that we are but dust—dust infused with divinity, but still dust. And we strain against the dichotomy of what we are and what we yearn to be.

In addition, many of us carry the emotional baggage of shame: the remorse over not what we **have done,** but who we **are.** We may feel corrupt, vitiated, at the very core of our beings. Some well-meaning but emotionally destructive parents, teachers, friends have warped our sense of self, have damaged our egos, have helped us— often unknowingly—develop feelings of inadequacy, even self-loathing. A lifetime of successes and accomplishments cannot eradicate the stigma of toxic shame. It cannot restore the shredded selfhood that some of us experienced in our childhood and have had reinforced by others during strategic

periods in our lives. The most poisonous barbs to self-esteem, however, come from the unrelenting critic which lives in our hearts, mercilessly castigating us. That critic—sometimes a whole committee of detractors—is the menacing voice of a misguided self. True health and happiness, we gradually learn, rests in embracing and transforming that dishonored self into a loving, accepting one.

But before that happens, that dishonored self is reluctant, even unable--to trust others because of past disappointments: a recognition of others' perfidy, a remembrance of earlier disillusionment; and it becomes more understandable why healthy self-esteem is rare. Our failure to value ourselves springs from being trapped in a pit of lonely despair, from being treated with obvious contempt and rejection, from soul-deep pain inflicted by those who professed to love us. We protect ourselves from a whole-hearted, generous giving of ourselves and all our abilities to God, and to normal friendly relationships with others, because we fear we will be hurt yet again, as we have been wounded so often in the past.

Whether from guilt, remorse, traumatic experiences of the past, or countless other internal or external circumstances, many of us **do not value ourselves**. And in de-valuing self, we tend to de-value our neighbors, also, and fail to give God the glory and praise due Him. In effect, we break the First Commandment because we do not recognize God as God.

If we did obey that commandment, we would recognize Divine omnipotence, Divine unconditional love, Divine indwelling in all His creatures. We are made in the image of God: we carry the God-life within us: and, metaphysically speaking, that God is **all Act**. We are Potentiality—waiting to become our true selves, waiting for God to act in us. And God, Eternal Mother/Father, continually engenders us: continually creates and re-creates us anew according to Her plan and as far as we allow.

We are the Beloved of God. Right this minute God loves us with a complete, irrevocable, all-encompassing love. Despite our weaknesses, failings, and pallid acknowledgement of that love, God loves us. How that certainty stirs our souls--how we long to be assimilated in that love!

Yet how weak and frail is our response in times of trouble or doubt. All too readily we let go of that certainty; all too quickly do we sink into the quagmire of depression and discouragement. Confused and depressed in that insidious maelstrom, we lose sight of our Beloved and our belovedness; we withdraw into ourselves instead of abandoning ourselves to God's care, instead of trusting in Divine Providence. Rather than relying on Him, we allow ourselves to fall into the dark abyss of our nothingness, where only misery lurks.

How can we strengthen this lackluster love of self? Sometimes it seems that the longest distance in the universe is the one that stretches interminably between head and heart, convictions and feelings. How can we make truly our own what we profess to believe?

One certain way, of course, is to search for and embrace the truth. In times of depression, anxiety, and discouragement, we cannot trust ourselves. We are not thinking aright; we must trust another to guide us—not to tell us what to do as much as help us acknowledge and follow the light within. When we seek others' help, we find—if we are fortunate—someone who will listen to us, someone who will help us find the God Who lives deep in the recesses of our souls. We have but to open ourselves to the illumination which can dispel our darkness, bringing warmth to our frigidity, torrents of grace to our desert, and fruitfulness to our barrenness. So the first requirement on the road to self-love is humility to admit our need, then to articulate it to one whom we trust to point out the way to Truth.

Somewhere, somehow, our fragile selves assimilated into our psyches a pernicious lie: we started to believe we were not good enough, not smart enough, not talented enough, not thin enough etc. Early on, we learned by a kind of psychological osmosis that we were failures in any one of a hundred realms. We believed it; we lived it; we let it color our self-image; we allowed it to permeate our relationships with others, although we did our best to hide our deficiencies as best we could. We over-compensated socially by becoming braggarts or bullies; we adopted an attitude of I-don't-care by engaging in arrogant, prideful behavior; we found solace in material things, more dependable than the people who—knowingly or not—hurt us and left us feeling worthless. This lie has affected our lives, and it is time to expose it for what it is: damnable and damning!

The Truth is that we are good, loving, and worthy of being loved. As an old saying has it: "God don't make no junk!" Another, more touching axiom declares, "God loves you so much He can't take His eyes off you!" Scripture abounds with the Truth: We are made in God's image; God loves us with an eternal, inexhaustible, unconditional love; we have been bought with a great price; our bodies are Temples of the Spirit; Christ loves us as the Father has loved Him. **That** is the Truth.

But it is often difficult to acknowledge the truth after we have discovered it. A story is told about a four-year-old child whose mother and older sister were teaching the youngster to jump rope. The mother and older sister applauded and cheered as the youngster tried and tried again, until finally the little girl announced proudly, "OK—I can do it by myself now," and self-confidently walked away. A little while later she returned disconsolately dragging her jump-rope and said, "Yes, I know how to do it—but I need a lot of clapping!"

And so does everyone. We need affirmation and approval, no matter what anyone has taught us: we not only <u>like,</u> we actually **need** the acceptance, affection, and approval of others. We thrive when someone sees something good in us—**and lets us know it.** No flowers need water and sunshine more than we need "a lot of clapping"! But how often do we admit our need; how often are we honest enough to let others know we are not the confident, self-sufficient, even arrogant persons we appear to be? No wonder they withhold approval: we seem to be getting along just fine without help from anybody!

Refusing to listen to the lies which denigrate us, seeking the Truth from a trusted source, allowing others to affirm and encourage us—these are all deterrents to an unhealthy, false betrayal of self. Are there other means—practical and practicable—which can lead us to the love of self which we deserve, and which God desires for us?

Acknowledging the truth about ourselves--that we are beloved of God, but weak, wounded, and flawed—is the first step. Next is Acceptance. We **accept** God's love, we **accept** our own vulnerability. We face reality, Truth. We adjust to what is, instead of being caught in the downward destructive spiral of criticism and complaint about ourselves or others. This is an **attitude**, and attitudes can be changed, adapted according to our desires. Someone asked, "What does a caterpillar have to do to become a butterfly?" The answer: "It must want to change so much that it is willing to leave the safety and familiarity of its chrysalis." No one says it is easy. But it is life-giving, and it leads to happiness. I must give up what I **am** in hope of becoming what I **could be.**

I must be willing to be changed, to accept the Will of God for me. And what God wills is **good.** My overbearing attitude, my self-complacency, my illusion of self-sufficiency, my angry outbursts or critical comments—these are not good for me or for anyone else. I become willing to relinquish such defeating behavior, admitting my culpability and begging for the grace to change. Gradually, in God's time, He will change me; He will do for me what I cannot do for myself.

"The abyss that is my soul invokes unceasingly the abyss that is my God," Silesius wrote centuries ago. Even before that, Augustine had exclaimed, "Thou has made us for thyself, O Lord, and our hearts are restless until they rest in thee." Today we acknowledge that same yearning for the Divine. The flame of God-life within us burns in ardent desire to be united to its Source. A healthy self-love is a step towards that union.

Thanksgiving Day

St. Paul prays, thanking God for the graces bestowed on us and wishing us peace, reminding us that God is faithful, and calling us to fellowship with Jesus Christ. And remember the Gospel's familiar story of the ten lepers, one of whom returned to give thanks, earning from Jesus the consoling words, "Your faith has saved you."

Gratitude, faith, peace, and joy: these are the virtues emphasized in today's liturgy. They are inextricably linked, I think, with peace and joy flowing from the first two. Many of us are deeply grateful for the peace and joy that have often flooded our souls, even as we prayerfully beg for the same in our troubled world. Some of that peace comes from an acknowledgement of our imperfections, our vulnerability, an admission of our absolute need for God. As G. K. Chesterton wrote, "We're all in the same boat, and we're all sea-sick." We are all essentially alike: we need God; we need each other. We desperately want a remedy for our particular sickness. Inner peace follows not the remedy, which may be a long, long time coming, but the humble recognition that we are weak, broken.

As a client prepares to depart from Guest House after undergoing treatment there, she plans a small gift for those whom she leaves. When my treatment time was over, I decided to buy each one a little stone imprinted with a relevant word or phrase: "One day at a time" or "Recovery" or "Patience," etc. I was in a hurry, so I simply took a couple handfuls of the stones, and asked the clerk to count out thirty of them.

As I selected a stone and wrote an accompanying note to each Sister, I came across a lovely green one that was unfortunately imperfect. It read only "Blessed be." "Too bad!" I thought. "It **should** say 'Blessed be God' or 'Blessed be the name of Jesus' or something like that." So I kept the defective stone for myself—I wouldn't give someone else such an incomplete thing.

It has taken a while, but gradually it is dawning on me: the **stone** wasn't defective; my thinking was! In every moment of life we can say **Blessed be.** For each person we love or who loves us; every challenge we face, each heartache, each bit of happiness, **Blessed be!** Each opportunity we have to share, to listen, to laugh, to **BE**: **Blessed be!**

If we have faith to see that, we will be grateful; and we will experience peace and joy. With an attitude of gratitude, we accept each person, place, thing, event, or circumstance as coming from the hands of our loving God, and we say: **Blessed be!**

And now, as we prepare to enter more deeply into the liturgy, we experience again the glory and wonder of Christ coming to us. **Faith** tells us that in Bethlehem, He became our brother; at Calvary, He became our ransom; here, on our altar, He becomes our food. **Blessed be** this Holy Table, where we become what we receive: the Body of Christ, Eucharist—Beautiful Gift--for each other. What else could be an appropriate response except a **Joyous Thanksgiving.**

Ten (Plus One) Commandments for Teachers

    I.   Thou shalt respect the God-light in each student, especially when it seems to be obscured or even extinguished altogether. Thou shalt also respect confidentiality in all thy dealings with students unless prudence dictates otherwise.

   II.   Thou shalt learn each student's name within the first week of classes, and shalt call her or him by that name as often as possible, for there is no sound on earth sweeter than thine own name spoken in a friendly tone. Thou shalt not permit derogatory or discriminatory nicknames, however. Thou shalt call her Florence, not Fatty; Stephen, not Stinky etc. Under no circumstances shalt thou tolerate discrimination of any kind.

  III.   Thou shalt not seek to engage in a popularity contest. Thy students do not want or need thee as a pal, but as a mentor, a guide, a constant and sure source of strength and wisdom. Therefore, thou shalt keep thy personal business to thyself: thy age, boy/girl friends, irrrelevant facts or opinions, etc. Thou art a professional. However, thou shalt **love** thy students—whether thou feelest like it or not—without sentimentality or exclusion.

  IV.   Thou shalt not threaten, cajole, coax, or bribe thy students by fair means or foul—and this verily includeth (but is not restricted to) the bestowal of marks or grades, which are to be exceedingly fair, just, and objective.

   V.   Thou shalt try with all thy strength to give honest praise and recognition to   students for anything good they may   do, remembering thine may be the only encouraging voice they heareth all day.

VI. Thou shalt be extremely careful and circumspect about every promise thou dost make; whatever it is, thou **MUST** fulfill it; therefore, it behooveth thee to think thrice before thou dost make one.

VII. Thou shalt look at thyself in thy mirror each day and say to thyself, "Thou art a teacher; the love of God shineth through thee to bless and guide youth; thy students depend on thee for learning, affirmation, and support." Then thou shalt act accordingly.

VIII. Thou shalt try by every means available to make thy classes interesting, lively, and fun; however, thou shalt expect appropriate diligence, study, and memorization as well as understanding and appreciation.

IX. Remembering that the egos of thy students are extremely fragile, thou shalt precede every correction with a positive statement about her or him. Furthermore, thou shalt not expect teenagers to act, think, or feel like adults.

X. Above all, thou shalt **pray** daily both for thyself and for thy students.

XI. (extra credit) Thou shalt never, **never**, *never* assign an essay as "punishment.

Preaching X3

(Racine Dominican Sisters Jean Ackerman, Mary Fisher, and Emily Oszewski (who died shortly afterward: **R.I.P.***) arranged to meet informally one summer evening to share ideas about the Dominican charism of preaching. Shall we listen as they converse?)*

"What a lovely setting for a conference!" Emily exclaimed as she settled on one of the park benches dotting the lawn at Siena Center.

"Not a real conference," Mary noted, "just an informal sharing." She, too, seated herself on a bench overlooking the calm lake.

"As I look out over Lake Michigan," Jean said, standing and gazing at it, "I remember this past Good Friday in Willmar, Minnesota. A parishioner asked me, 'Why do we venerate a cross instead of a crucifix? When will Jesus be placed back on the cross?'"

"How did you answer, Jean?" Emily leaned forward curiously.

Jean sat, then replied meditatively, "I thought the question demanded a response of integrity and purpose, so I told him that when we venerate the cross, we enter into the pain and anguish of suffering people everywhere-past, present, and to come. We reverence the grief and sorrow of those who are hurting, confused, violated..."

"Her voice grew husky with emotion, and she paused a moment before continuing. "When we venerate the cross, we enter the Paschal mystery more fully as we witness Christ's unconditional embrace of these horrendous sufferings throughout history. And we believe that because He embraced, then conquered the cross, our crosses, too, will lead to new life, to a transforming experience."

Birds twittered, loud in the sudden silence. Mary hesitatingly began after a moment, "I know what you mean. For years, as I have done pulpit preaching, I have taken to heart the belief that we preach more effectively by our daily lives than we do with words. Until recently, however, I did not fully understand that I can preach, too, through acknowledgement of my weakness."

Emily responded with animation, "Mary, that's one of my certainties: that our efforts to seek God's presence in every detail of life is the core of our preaching and living! But could you explain your new understanding a little more ?"

"I hope so," she replied with a slight smile. "I have had many personal difficulties, which sent me for treatments to Guest House. It was there that I was blessed with the honesty, openness, and willingness to admit the truth about myself: I am-and always will be--an addict. I am not like 'normal' people: I have a specific disease, an incurable, terminal condition. This is my cross; and I need help if I am to carry it successfully."

Excitedly, Jean interrupted, " That's exactly what I meant! Such spiritual issues need to be addressed by Dominican--by all--

preachers today! I believe such issues are about integration of life--
of achieving balance and harmony in dealings with others and
ourselves. How can we preach resurrection without the cross?
People everywhere must be helped to realize that the Paschal
mystery continues to enfold us in our time and place. We're not
living in enclosed glass houses or in cozy little cocoons. Spirituality
separated from the realities of life is not an option for us! But--
please go on."

Mary paused, looked at the clouds as if for inspiration, then
continued, "As I admit my vulnerability, my brokenness, I hope I am
living and preaching the Paschal mysteries. When I acknowledge
my flawed humanity, no longer need I pretend to be confident, self-
assured, superior; with Christ I have died--and the dead have no
power. But I joyfully relinquish my illusion of power to allow
Christ's power to live and work through me.

"I experience great peace and serenity in claiming my woundedness.
Then I become more aware of other suffering people--people who
call for my care and concern, who need me as much as I need them,
and through whom Christ also exercises His life-giving power."

"You are mentioning a facet of contemplation," Emily added.
"Basically, it involves allowing   the Spirit of Wisdom to operate in
us, leading us to recognize the presence of God in the humdrum, the
commonplace, even the pain in our lives and in the suffering people
of the world, and then to reflect that in our preaching."

"Yes, that's true," Jean commented eagerly. "Our preaching moves from a historic re-telling of the gospel to an integrated connection with the Risen Christ, with the Cosmic Christ, with whom we are joined today in our reality."

And it is in our efforts to see God's presence in every detail of life that the core of our preaching will develop into the living Word of God," Emily noted, with discernible reverence.

"I know my companions may not realize I am preaching; often I may not realize it, either," Mary continued. "But when I accept myself as I am while trying to be the woman God wants me to be, I am united--along with everyone else who wills to be united--to the Suffering Savior, Jesus Christ. Together with Him and with all of humanity, I bear the agonies of my addiction, its consequent struggles, and every other cross, in union with the Crucified One. With Him, we hope for a Resurrection into a new and glorious life."

Jean and Emily nodded their heads, and the latter spoke with great sincerity. "That attitude comes from a spirit of contemplation, which includes both contemplative prayer and contemplative living, as I mentioned earlier. They mutually support and foster each other."

"But--" asked Mary, "how can we strengthen this spirit in ourselves and convince our busy brothers and sisters to incorporate contemplation into their sometimes frenetic lives?"

Emily sat straighter as she declared with conviction, "Even the busiest--perhaps **especially** the busiest among us need the support of contemplative prayer. Those who minister in situations that are overwhelming cannot long survive without the life-replenishment provided by the contemplative stance. It is out of contemplation that our true love and justice grow."

"I agree," Jean assented. "And I think the place of contemplation in our contemporary lives must be continually revitalized, contrary to the dictates of our consumer-driven society.

"My challenge as a preacher is to be grounded in contemplative stance, to breathe in the God Presence and keep focused clearly on why I preach even a single sentence. If I neglect my contemplative life, I forfeit my charism of preaching my piece of the truth."

Emily extended her arms as she surveyed the scenic beauty around her. "Look at all this," she invited. "In our preaching we are called to proclaim God's goodness as we learn it in our prayer, to be beacons of hope in the darkness of world situations, to help others look beneath the surface and see how great is our God."

"That is the joyful privilege of the preacher," Mary asserted. "And our preaching can sometimes be challenging, too."

"You're right," agreed Jean. "Preaching is challenging for the preacher as well as for any faith community. It calls for courageous hearts and strong convictions about preaching a Just Word. It requires also the willingness to experience conversion and transformation of lives.

"I am convinced," she went on, "about the call of Dominican preachers to be prophetic witnesses who consume the Word of God and then 'make bold proclamation' as the Acts of Apostles says about the disciples. How bold are we in our proclamations? Why should we hesitate? Have we not been set free through the suffering, death, and resurrection of Christ?"

"That prospect sometimes worries me," Mary confessed. "I don't want to be challenging or admonishing good, sincere people-- 'preaching to the choir' as it's called. I choose not to tell others what to do as much as to encourage them to search their own hearts for the answers deep within.

"Personally, I have always been more stirred to conversion by hearing of God's unconditional love and mercy, by the thought of God as my Beloved, Whom I encounter daily in manifestations of Beauty in art, music, literature, poetry, and drama. When I share my experiences, appreciation, and insights, I think this, too, is preaching."

"I understand; I, too, use the arts, especially music, as complementing more formal preaching," Jean agreed. "But often, perhaps in social settings, at staff gatherings, or on the phone-- personal opportunities for preaching outside of more formal occasions--there are times when I need the courage to speak out when I know my message is not always the hoped-for, expected, or popular answer.

"In more formal opportunities, too: at liturgies, public prayer, Communion Services, I am privileged to express my preaching charism. Preaching in a faith community through RCIA presentations and weekly breaking open the Word with catechumens and candidates is a touching example of sharing insights and inspirations."

The others murmured in assent and appreciation, until..."Oh!" Emily exclaimed, gesturing toward the sky, "How gorgeous!" All three gazed at the multi-colored ribbons stretching across the heavens.

Jean broke the awed silence by remarking, "I pray that we keep in our preaching a visionary and creative edge, which lights fires both in the preacher and in those who listen. God's spirit can burst forth from the printed word just as these vibrant colors paint the heavens."

"Let us pray for each other--and for all preachers," suggested Emily, "that we may be open to the Spirit and passionate in our response to the infinite, unconditional love of God." After a few minutes of fervent silent prayer, the trio concluded by praising God's goodness manifested in the beauty of the sunset.

Part IV: Introduction:
Glimpse of an Addicted Woman

As you will read, I spent six and a half months
at Guest House in Lake Orion, Michigan,
an excellent treatment center for women religious.
*Therapist **Anne Sutherland, M. Ed., CAC-1,***
*and **Dr.Douglas MacDonald**,*
chief among others, have been my counselors,
advisers, and friends. I can never thank
or praise them enough for helping me
begin to change my attitudes
and manage my emotions.
I include here copies of the letters I wrote to my
community from Guest House.
I hope reading them will encourage you to
pray for all addicted people
and for their therapists, especially for
the dedicated personnel at Guest House

Foreword

Why would anyone want to read about someone else's addiction? I can think of several reasons:

- ❖ *Misery loves company.*
- ❖ *We can say 'Well, I'm not as bad as <u>she</u> was!"*
- ❖ *It will give us something to talk about at the water cooler, Laundromat, bridge table, PTA meeting, church social, self-help group session, diet club, etc.*
- ❖ *Furthermore, since this particular book has been written by a Dominican Sister (a "nun" in common terms) there may be additional motives for reading;*
    - ○ *I never thought of the Sisters having such mundane problems, of being <u>human,</u> just like us.*
    - ○ *How could she develop such a problem in a convent, where she was supposed to be practicing virtue?*

But there might be some who will read these pages to learn something, to come in touch with their own humanity while reading about others' weaknesses. It is in that hope that I offer this part of my little book, to share parts of my life-long struggle with **eating**.

Whatever your reason, I thank you for being willing to read my story

Dear Sisters,   December 8, 2000

No, this is NOT a photo of Guest House, but it's the best representation I can find right now.

Our ride here was both challenging and delightful: challenging because of the weather and road conditions (We averaged 25 mph during the first four hours) and delightful because of the Dominican companionship and cheerful camaraderie Joyce, Maggie, and I shared.

When we finally arrived at Guest House just before locking-up time at 10 PM, we discovered a mansion-like structure that hinted of former opulence. Some remnants of past glory remain: dark walnut or cherry wood paneling, fireplaces, exquisitely carved pieces of furniture, and—get this: the dining room ceiling is made from white elephant hide! We used a rickety ancient cage elevator (Remember 1209 Park Avenue?), temperamental but still serviceable, to transport my suitcases, bags, and bundles up to Room 14 on the second floor, where I was pleasantly surprised—even overwhelmed—by the accommodations.

My bedroom is larger than the one I left behind in E-Wing, and boasts a walk-in closet, a private bathroom, a double bed with a luxurious mattress, as well as a matched set of desk, chest of drawers, night and telephone stands, and padded rocker. A comfortable recliner and a footrest with storage space are positioned so I can look out the expansive bay windows offering a view of the front entrance, with dozens of trees (but no lake!) in the background.

I was scheduled for three meetings with various staff-members this morning, but for one reason or another, all three were cancelled. The therapist/counselor/mentor who has been assigned to me (or vice versa) is Anne Sutherland; the other clients tell me I am very fortunate to be under her care and guidance. She has been ill; in addition, she lives out in the country someplace, and roads are impassible because of yesterday's snow storms. But I'm sure we'll get together soon. Please pray that it will be a profitable association, and that I may learn a lot of humility, patience, and mildness even before we meet.

So far I've met a cloistered Dominican from Farmington Hills, Michigan; a Felician from New Jersey, and a Dominican from Sinsinawa—all good women, all cordial and welcoming. Thanks to Sister Therese's industry, I have use of this computer—at least for a while; I am grateful for the opportunity to send a message your way. A therapist joined us for breakfast this morning and frowned when we talked about connecting the computer and printer. Quite officiously she discouraged me from expecting to use it:

"Are you looking for special treatment on your very first day?" she asked, with eyebrows raised, nose elevated, lips pursed. I took an instant dislike to her. Lord forgive me! Making snap judgments is NOT the way to win friends and influence people, and **definitely not** the way to initiate a peaceful relationship. So I must try with great resolve to watch my step with X.

Let us continue to pray for each other!

December 16, 2000

Dear Sisters,

SNOWED IN !!!!

Here's the week in review:

<u>Monday, the 11th</u>:   During a special celebration honoring a Felician leaving Guest House, we sang in her honor. Her favorite tune is "The Yellow Rose of Texas," so the ditty went something like this:

New Jersey is the home of Sister Mary Fran;
She's going back to Lodi as quickly as she can.
She's shined her shoes and packed her bags
'Cuz now she's heading home;
And once she's safely settled there,
She never more will roam.

When a Sister leaves there's great festivity: Mass for her intentions, a gift from the others ($1 from each) and a dinner of her favorite foods. Today we feasted on fresh asparagus spears, steak, baked potatoes with cheese, lemon cheese cake for dessert. An after-dinner ceremony honored the "graduate." It was extremely impressive and touching.

<u>Tuesday, the 12th</u>:   I was to have my first-ever appointment with a psychologist, and I wanted to make a good first impression. I bathed with special care, set my hair so I wouldn't look like the Wild Woman of Borneo, even used a little talcum—not much, just a touch of mysteriously elusive fragrance. I donned my black dress with

touches of red and blue (dignified, but not somber) and felt ready for the Great Adventure. Regrettably, all appointments have been cancelled because of the heavy snowfall.

Last night when the TV reports centered around the snow pile-ups in the Detroit area (Center Line, Warren, Sterling Heights, Dearborn were mentioned), I said, "I love hearing those familiar names again!" I was thinking about my friends and relatives in those suburbs, the good times we had shared, etc. Sister W. snarled, "And I *hate* them! I hate Lake Orion and Guest House and everything in Michigan! I wish I had never heard of this place!" I kept quiet, surprised at her bitter vehemence.

The next morning at breakfast she said to me," I'm sorry—I didn't mean anything personal in my comments about Michigan. It's just that I have been **_forced_** by my community to come here, and I hate everything about the place." Sisters, please pray for Sister W. I don't know what her addiction is—she's a small, wiry woman in her 70's—but it must be very painful for her to be here. Please pray that W. finds help, acceptance, love, and peace in the healing process that Guest House offers.

Sister A. was born and raised in County Cork, Ireland, and every time I hear her delightful brogue I think of our Brenda. Sister L. comes from Kenya—"just a bit away from Kisumu," she says. I know all the Sisters' names now, but not their stories. Perhaps that will come later, in our group sessions. This afternoon—a day free of classes, lectures, and exercises because staff members could not travel the snowy, icy roads—I played Scrabble with the cloistered Dominican and a Sister of Charity who is a counselor for alcohol-

and drug-addicts. Yes, she is one of the "clients" here. As one of the nurses said, "Even intellectuals can be helped by our program. It just takes them longer!"

Forgive me for inundating you with messages—I know the bulletin board is always full. But I miss you, and writing even a few silly lines makes me feel I am with you, at least **now**.

<u>Wed., Dec. 13th</u>: I had a shock during my physical exam: Dr. Coleman told me I am now in Congestive Heart Failure! All this gasping for breath, tiredness, back and chest pain is due to CHF: both lungs and my heart have retained fluid. My medications were changed and increased; I was given orders to rest and *rest* and **rest.** I asked if this would jeopardize my being accepted into the program, and was assured that since the condition can be controlled and monitored, I am still a candidate. (Yes, that makes me happy, because I think GH will help me be a better person.)

<u>Thurs. and Fri., Dec. 14th and 15th:</u> I rested and rested and rested, except for attending the special Mass and Farewell Ceremony for Jackie Lathers, R. N., who has been the chief nurse here for more than sixteen years. It was Jackie, along with Sister Mae, who—five or six years ago—was chiefly responsible for converting the program at Guest House from the care of religious men to the care of religious women, after convincing church authorities that there was such a need. They call her the "heart" of GH; she is the one who encourages residents to "expect a miracle." During the farewell party for her, attended by more than 72 guests (**All** of whom, it seemed to me, wanted to give a speech!) residents sang a song to the tune of "Take me out to the Ballgame":

Jackie, I have a headache; Jackie, my throat is sore.
Give me some Advil or Tylenol so I won't hurt anymore.
Arthritic bones are a-creakin'—They need something for sure;
Please, dear Jackie, please help as I stand at your door.

It went on for 3, 689 more stanzas—No, really for only four more, all in the same vein, but with different emergencies. Smiles glimmered among the tears.

Long tables with white tablecloths and linen napkins had been set up in both wings of the Great Hall, with floral centerpieces and candles. The "legal meal" (Everyone at GH is served the same menu) consisted of baked potatoes, Cornish hens, vegetables, fresh rolls and FRESH RASPBERRIES!

<u>Sat., Dec. 16th</u>: I was feeling strong and **rested** enough to do my laundry and read a little. I also had an interview with lovable Dr. Doug MacDonald, a specialist in about a million medical matters., especially addictions. He told me I am "normal." (I asked for a signed affidavit to testify to that, but he demurred.) Among comments he made was the following:

If you have a group of 100 people representing various cultures, backgrounds, and personalities, and you ask how many of them <u>overeat</u> when they are stressed, lonely, bored, or upset, 50% of them will raise their hands. Then if you ask how many of them are <u>unable to eat </u>when they are stressed, lonely, bored, or upset, the other 50% will raise their hands.

When I admitted that I eat, not because something is nutritious, but because it tastes good, he said, "Food is **supposed** to taste good. God made it that way!" So instead of the scolding or ridiculing I was expecting, I received understanding and encouragement. God bless him!!!

194

Dear Sisters,   December 17, 2000

It's so *quiet* here—no paging, no phones ringing, only subdued talking in the dining room—I feel as if I'm on a retreat! I miss you all, and find myself converting EST to CST, then wondering what you are doing at that particular time. I face the direction leading toward Siena Center and join you in spirit.

Some of the Sisters have gone to the movies; some are building a snowman; others are clearing the walks; some are writing out their weekly reports. I continue to rest—and that's getting b-o-r-i-n-g !

You may be interested to know that one of the Sisters here has a relative who spent time in a Canadian monastery with Alex Trebeck of "Jeopardy" fame. Another one worked for 12 years with Dan Crosby, OFM Cap., in Wyoming. Several have asked about Sisters Kathy Thomas and Maria Orlando. One is a Dominican from Mission San Jose, California.

It's a rule of the house that we do not ask personal questions of each other: last name, community, ministry, etc., so that anonymity and privacy may be preserved. But some volunteer more information than others do. I'm the only one known by my full name; I just automatically introduce myself as *Sister Mary Fisher,* although some are a little startled that I do. *"Whatthehay,"* I think, *"Anyone looking at me can see that I've got a problem. I can't hide xxx pounds!"*

195

They tell me that "art classes" are offered a few days every week. I was hoping for a tour of the house, with a study of the fascinating architecture, carvings, stained-glass and leaded windows, upholstered chairs, etc., but I learned that they are really not art classes, but crafts. In the spirit of the day, I say *Bah! Humbug!*

The last classes have been doing "busy work" of fashioning Christmas ornaments or seasonal cards. No comment. But I shall have to satisfy my curiosity another way.

At a recent meal, one of the Sisters offered another, "I'll give you all my mashed potatoes for half of your meat loaf." And a trade was effected. I'd have given up the potatoes, meat loaf, and the whole table of fresh vegetables for a couple of Marlene's cookies!

By the way, I have finally seen—though not actually met—the woman who will be my counselor/therapist/mentor and what-ever-the-heck-else-she-is-supposed-to-be. She's an attractive woman with the darkest, most beautiful eyes I have ever seen. Her hair, too, worn simply, is jet black, so I wonder if she has some Indian blood in her. The way she moves reminds me of a dancer or athlete—you know, that sort of half-dance, all energy and movement, and a *Laissez le bon temps rouler* attitude. I bet she's a lot of fun when she isn't therapy-ing or counsel-ing or mentor-ing. I hope we get along. I am determined to do **my** part. (I just hope she doesn't pry!) (or preach at me) (or scold me) (or treat me like a child) (or bawl me out) (or.........sigh. I guess I'm expecting way too much. I should expect some confrontation, I guess. Nobody ever promised me a rose garden.....)

Let us continue to pray for each other. I'm feeling blue, lonesome, very much alone. I wish I had someone to talk to—and not about addictions! I'm sick unto death of that subject! Enough is enough. Besides that, doggone it, **I'm hungry!!!!! And I'm not yet officially in the program.** Who knows what torments will follow? I'm getting nervous and apprehensive and just plain scared! I'd whistle a happy tune, as the song suggests, but I can't whistle! This is one of those times I should be saying Acts of Faith and Trust and Resignation and Humility and Obedience and all the other virtues I lack. So--as I wrote at the beginning of this paragraph--please pray for me!

December 21, 2000
Dear Sisters,

I thank you with all my heart for all the lovely messages you have sent me. My heart overflows with gratitude for your gracious remembrances. I read and re-read each note and letter, and will read them all a third and fourth time, undoubtedly even oftener, especially on Christmas Day.

They will help to make up for a number of recent disappointments. I was refused permission to get my hair cut. "Your health is too fragile," the staff said. I was refused permission to attend a family party on Sunday afternoon. "Your health is too fragile," they decided again. I may not even be permitted to attend Mass on Christmas Day because of that same reason. I must learn to accept and even rejoice in God's Providence; I am glad I have your notes to bolster my spirits.

Counselors and nurses are very kind, even if a trifle over-solicitous or cautious. Stubborn and independent as I am, **I** want to be the one in control of my life. But since I haven't done such a good job of it in the past, I must learn to accept and abide by others' decisions. (Darn it!) I have moved to another room, the bedroom suite that millionaire Scripps had designed and built for his mother. The corner room, it offers views to the north and west, and is spacious to the point of luxury, with a separate dressing room, mirrored make-up table, extensive closets, etc. The bathroom has both a tub and a glass-enclosed, walk-in shower; it is decorated with the famous Pewabic tile on walls and floor. "Age has it privileges," I tell lthe other Sisters who tease me about being "The Queen Mother," now living in the high-rent district.

Today the scheduled priest was not able to come to celebrate Mass with us because of the snowy roads. We are usually fortunate, having the Liturgy on 11 AM weekdays and at 5 PM on Saturdays. Several different priests come from the Men's Guest House a few miles away. When one said "We addicts..." during a homily, I felt as the people in Molokai must have felt when Father Damien identified himself with the lepers. We had anointing of the sick last week during Mass, private confessions yesterday, and anticipate a special Advent service at 4:30 this afternoon, just before dinner. There are considerable opportunities for private prayer and reflection, and I feel as if I am on an extended retreat or sabbatical, and am very grateful for these spiritual benefits.

On December 7, just before leaving Siena Center, I found a small box of raisins which some kind person had placed in my mail box. I resolved to save it until I was really desperate for food. Today is Raisin Day. Thank you, dear Anonymous Donor!

My prayers for you at this holy time is that God will grant you all that is infinitely good, eternally true, and divinely beautiful. Please continue to hold me in your prayers, too. Every day I realize how much I need God.

Thank you again for writing. I need you; I appreciate you and everything you are and all you do! Have a Blessed, Merry Christmas!

No, no meeting yet with the elusive Miss Sutherland. Of course, I'm not officially in the Program yet, so ---But I get more and more scared with each passing day. I've been hearing some horror stories about the rules and regulations here, and about the ones who dare to criticize or disobey. Woe is me! Something tells me I'm in for a more difficult time than I had expected. Come to think of it, I hadn't expected anything like Guest House at all. Oh, everyone is friendly and affable on the surface, but I fear what dark and dastardly deeds they are planning for us when they remove their velvet gloves and really get down to business. So far, it's been the life of Reilly for me. All I do is rest and pray and eat (I use the term loosely..... "snack" is more like it!) I have read more novels in these weeks than I have in the **last year** at Siena Center!) and watch sappy TV shows, the alternative to resting (again, yet, still!!!!) alone in my room.

But I am putting on a good show. I look pleasant, act sociably, smile a lot. I feel like the "Shadow" --you know: "Who knows what evil lurks in the hearts of men? The <u>Shadow</u> knows!!!"! And his fiendish laugh: "Hahahahahaha......!"

I wish I had something interesting **TO DO** !

New Year's Day, 2001

Dear Sisters,

It's official! I have been accepted as a client at Guest House! It's also official: I now weight sixteen pounds less than when I left Racine. Of course there's a price: I am ready to pounce upon and devour **anything** that isn't alive and moving!

As a regular "client," I now fill out a special paper after each meal, recording what was eaten, how much, and where it belongs in the Pyramid Food Plan. When my cousin called and asked if we had a good New Year's dinner, I replied, "I don't remember the food exactly, but it contained 3 ounces of protein, 2 servings of carbohydrates, 2 fruits, 2 vegetables, and ½ serving of fat." Who could ask for anything more?

We had a lovely service in chapel on Christmas Eve. After appropriate carols and prayers, leaders distributed vigil lights in clear glass holders, along with a fresh match. We were asked to step up to the statue of the Christ Child in the middle of our circle and announce our prayer intentions. I asked for prayers for my "beloved Racine Dominican community, for my family and friends." Then I— and each one in turn—lit the wax candle and placed the vigil light on the red velvet cloth on which the Infant lay. After more prayers, each claimed her vigil light and left chapel holding it while singing and processing to the dining room.   There we were treated to a sumptuous feast of celery, carrot, and zucchini sticks; cauliflower and broccoli flowerets, and yes—even <u>radishes!</u> ***Yummy!***

Some of us went to the basement lounge afterwards to reminisce about other Christmases. At 11:45 we were startled out of our remembrances by the **_FIRE ALARM!_** You guessed it: one of the Sisters had taken her vigil light upstairs and had fallen asleep. (Groggy, no doubt, from all the rich food!) A small fire in her bedroom was quickly extinguished while we huddled together in the appointed meeting place. The good news: ALL of us—some awakened from sleep—managed to meet there in less than four minutes. Better news: Sister A. firmly resolves NEVER to take vigil lights to her room again!

The past week has flown by, as all the weeks do. Every day after breakfast we have an hour-long lecture, then a ten-minute break, followed by an hour meeting, then Mass and lunch. After lunch there are "art" classes, exercises, individual conferences, assignments to complete, and doctors' appointments to keep.

Do I enjoy all this? Well, it's similar to going through the Novitiate again. What was tolerable for a 16-year-old, however, affects a septuagenarian drastically differently. And, although my therapist Anne is by far the best teacher, I wish I could be on her side of the lectern instead of sitting on the receiving end of a lecture, no matter how well it is presented. Nonetheless, I am grateful for this opportunity for growth of mind and spirit, though it's not all peaches and cream. (OOPS—I just typed a bad word!)

Every Friday we have the opportunity to spend the afternoon at a spa, with water-aerobic exercises, physical fitness equipment, Jacuzzi and sauna for our use. I haven't been allowed to participate yet; maybe after my breathing improves, I will accompany the others in one of the vans. Yes, I have a bathing suit, custom-designed by the Michigan Tent and Awning Company.

I cannot tell you how grateful I am for your cards, notes, messages. I treasure each one, and re-read each several times before propping it up on the windowsill. **Thank you!**

February 7, 2001
Dear Sisters,

Here is a Valentine's Day rose for my dear community; I hope it will speak to you of my love and appreciation for your prayerful support and concern.

I can't tell you how touched I was by your beautiful gesture of sending your prayers and blessings to me across the lake; when I told the other Sisters here about it, they, too, were moved. And they reminded me that I should be grateful for my loving community.

Yesterday I went back to my familiar neighborhood in Dearborn— about 50 minutes' drive from Guest House. I have been having problems, and asked to see a dentist. To my surprise and delight, the staff made arrangements for a ride to Dr. L's office. While I was there, I had the oddest feeling that somehow I was there more for him than for myself.

He asked me when and why I had left Wisconsin, so I told him about Guest House and its treatment for addicts of various kinds. Then he said, "I've been fighting my own battles with the bottle lately," and I thought, "AHA! That's why he looks so dissipated and old!" I told him some of the things I had learned about addictions, and assured him of my concern and prayers. I didn't scold or blame him, however, because I realize that accomplishes nothing except resentment. I hope God used me to plant a little seed in his mind and heart. Will you join me in praying for Dr. L., a good man struggling with alcoholism, shame, guilt, isolation, and anger?

Last Thursday I read aloud to the therapy group my "life story," complete with accounts of how my mis-use of food in times of stress had helped me form bad habits. I ended with my shock last October when the scale was perilously close to xxx. Then I told about my decision to ask for help from Guest House, and about the encouragement and understanding I received from all of you.

I wept during the reading of those nine typed pages; others wept, too. Afterwards, they commended me for my "honesty and courage." I learned that sharing secrets and weaknesses hidden for half a century can be therapeutic and life-giving when such sharing is received in a loving, non-judgmental manner. I hope I will be able to continue to do such sharing with YOU when I (finally! at long last! eventually!) leave here. Don't ask me _when._ I'm not supposed to ask that question. "Ours not to reason why / Ours but to do or die. . . ."

As of today, I have lost 27 pounds. They tell me that is NOT the most important thing, however. Instead, I am to ask myself, "Am I healthier in mind, body, and spirit? Am I learning how to deal with my emotions instead of burying them under a load of sweets? Am I closer to God and to my community?" To all, I answer a resounding YES!

The bane of my existence continues to be the daily group therapy sessions, which are a combination of Accusatory Chapter of Faults, the Spanish Inquisition, "Snake Pit," and the trial of Joan of Arc. So far, I have survived, *Deo gratias!* Maybe I should add the martyrdom of St. Lawrence to that list, because I felt as if I were on a hot griddle when it was my turn to be confronted!

Sunday I will be permitted to join a group going to see the movie, "Finding Forrester"—unless one of those !?#*?!#?!#dizzy spells rears its ugly head. I tell them there's nothing wrong with me that some of Marlene's cookies wouldn't cure. They think I'm kidding, but I'm not! My system still hasn't recovered from the shock of no sugar, no white flour, no caffeine, no cream etc., etc. etc.

I am glad I came here; I am grateful for your encouraging support, which enables me to stay. I hope I will come back to you a better— and healthier—member of the community, still bigger than average, but with a more positive attitude, a more loving heart, a greater capacity for compassionate understanding and acceptance. Please continue to pray that it may be so. Life is too short for any of us to neglect becoming the BEST we can be!

I am sending my very special Valentine's greetings to you—not any of that deep brown smooth stuff that slides down the throat so easily, not any of that stuff made with flour, margarine, sugar, baking powder, vanilla, and eggs; not any of those heart-shaped little things with clever saying on them; not even long-stemmed roses or carnations—I send you instead assurances of my love and prayers!

Brrrrrrrrrrrrrr!!!!

Dear Sisters,   February 11, 2001

It is a bright though cold day in Lake Orion; I hope you, too, are enjoying sunshine. Cheer up! We are closer to Spring than we were last month!

In a little while we will be having our weekly house meeting. At that time, we indicate our transportation needs for the week: visits to the doctor, dentist, hairdresser, shopping mall, movies etc. Then the acting secretary presents that list to the Staff on Monday. If the requests are approved, the appropriate arrangements are made with various drivers. It's a good system, and it works marvelously.

Our drivers are paid a trifling sum; their work is mostly contributive. Both men and women are employed, and I must admit I have my favorites. I do not always appreciate the risk-takers or the overly chatty ones, though I am grateful for the rides. Among the drivers are a retired dentist and a bank official, a television producer, grandmothers and grandfathers with time on their hands. They are all generous and courteous.

Once, after dropping off some argumentative Sisters at a K-Mart and continuing the trip with the rest of us, one driver was asked, "Does it bother you, Pat, when some of your passengers squabble a bit?"

"Oh, no," he answered; " I just act the way I do when my wife is in a bad mood: I turn off my hearing aid and don't pay any attention!"

Sometimes a request for transportation is not granted. If, for instance, someone addicted to <u>spending</u> exceeds the limit set by her counselor or borrows money from another Sister to buy something not previously planned upon, she may be denied shopping trips for a few weeks. Candy was found in the rooms of a few "guests," so their privileges were denied, too.

Once, a shopper left her companion (we are supposed to be "joined at the hip" with a partner whenever we go out) ostensibly to visit a restroom. She bought some liquor instead. *Fireworks ensued!* I am happy to report I have never broken the rules—yet! Please pray that I can keep that record unstained for the next few months!

This afternoon three of us are going to see "Cast Away." We are looking forward to the outing, even though we won't be able to get any popcorn to munch. We are allowed to see only those films with a PG-13 rating, and of those, only those without sex, violence, or references to alcohol or drugs. Pretty slim pickings nowadays!

When we bring videos into the house for our week-end viewing, the same rules apply. Some of the Sisters have been physically, emotionally, and/or sexually abused, and we try to keep a "safe" environment for all, so that no one will be exposed unnecessarily to unhappy reminders of her past.

The more I hear stories from the others, the more grateful I am for the calm, "ordinary" life I have led. I've had only problems dealing with emotions; imagine how I might have ballooned if I had had deeper conflicts! People would have called me "Two-ton Tessie" for sure!

And that reminds me: this afternoon some of us will be presenting "Prayers From the Arc" in our chapel. (I'm sure God will smile!) We will use a microphone so everyone can hear. I remember with fondness Siena's Noah, giraffe, monkey, little bird, cock, glow-worm, butterfly, dog, and dove. Best of all, however, I remember Sister Helen Arts' delight at representing the tortoise, with its heavy burden. I will reprise my role as the elephant and once more ask God that I may rejoice at all the lovable uniqueness of His marvelous creation.

Every week we answer questions regarding our progress and experiences here. Today I am handing in a paper which reports: "On two occasions marked by a difference of opinions I articulated my feelings and convictions calmly, without bombast or rancor; on another occasion I was actually meek and conciliatory." That should make them swallow their teeth in amazement!!

I also reported that my clothes are beginning to be a little too large—Hallelujah! It's a good thing Guest House has its own version of our Swap Shop. Here it's called "Our Daily Threads"; as women grow out of their clothes—one way or another—they donate items.

I finally received permission to join the exercise classes on Tuesdays and Thursdays. I was happy and excited, anticipating a great time, but I was amazed at how quickly I became tired. Following orders, I pranced for a while, then sat down and did chair exercises. After a while, I re-joined the "chorus line," then sat down—and so it went for the whole hour. There is a Sister here from Novia Scotia who astounds me by the gymnastics she is able to perform: sit-ups, back bends, full-body stretches—It's wonderful! I admire, but cannot emulate.

I really have to admire the women here--both clients and YES!--the counselors, instructors, therapists, staff personnel, etc. I'm sure that not one of them is here for the money--No one ever got rich by taking care of needy people, especially religious! I think they are dedicated, serious about wanting our recovery even more than we do--I bet they would like to knock our blocks off once in a while—or stick pins in a few effigies. Yes, even mine!!! I see so many flaws, weaknesses in others that I can't help wondering what they see in me. I guess we're all blind about ourselves. I learned something about the "Johari Window" which I will tell you about some time. Being here makes me look at myself seriously and honestly; what I see ain't so nice!

Dear Sisters,   February 25, 2001

By the time you read this, Lent will have begun. Let us pray for each
other that we may draw ever closer to our suffering Redeemer
during this holy season. I remember once reading a poem that had
as its refrain, "This year, my Jesus, let my <u>heart</u> keep Lent."

It doesn't seem like Lent here—it's more like the dead of winter.
Last night we had an ice storm with winds of up to 60 mph that
split branches from the trees, downed power lines, and blew
shingles off the roofs. The Sisters who have to walk over to the Villa
say that the grounds are full of broken branches, and they have to
pick their way carefully between them.

Did I ever mention that not all of the clients sleep in this big house?
Some of them—the younger, more limber ones—stay in a motel-like
structure on the grounds. They come here for all meals, classes, and
meetings, but they sleep over there. I don't envy them the walk on
dark, cold, icy nights and mornings!

Right now there are 24 residents at Guest House; this week, more
are arriving from all parts of the country for "After Care," a week-
long program of renewal for those who have "graduated" and are
now in Recovery. Space is at such a premium that the "After Care"
people—clients who have "graduated from GH and return for
periodic renewal times-- are being sent to local hotels for overnight
accommodations.

Another recent innovation of Guest House is the "half-way house"
now ready for recovering alcoholic priests. It is called "Nokomis,"

and I don't know why. The only Nokomis I know of is a character (I think) in Longfellow's <u>Hiawatha.</u> Does anyone know why that name would be given to such a house? At present three priests live there as they make their transition from a treatment center in Rochester, Minnesota, to the "real world" to which they will soon be going.

Yesterday our "Father Saturday," an amiable Jesuit from Nokomis, forgot he was supposed to say Mass in our chapel at 5 P.M. At 5:20, we started the liturgical readings, then had a Communion Service, during which Father Saturday showed up. Amid profuse apologies, he asked if he could return at 9 A.M. today. Of course we were very happy! This morning he gave an excellent homily, during which he was most kind, compassionate, and understanding. I was not surprised to learn he, too, is a "recovering" addict.

Last Thursday I presented my "Step One" to my therapy group. It is a searching examination of the place addiction has had in an individual's life: the secrets, shame, guilt, hopelessness, powerlessness etc. It was very difficult to dredge all those memories up from the last 75 years, and still more difficult to read the document to the others. But everyone (except one) was supportive, understanding, and encouraging.

The "old timers" here tell me that the hardest part is over once a client has presented Step One to the group. "It's all clear sailing from now on," they say. Step Two is an examination of how we "came to believe that a Power greater than ourselves could restore us to sanity" in handling our addictions. Sigh. Writing about that doesn't seem terribly easy to me right now!

Did you watch the TV production about the life of Judy Garland? I thought both actresses did a phenomenal job in portraying poor Judy. However, I wonder if any of you noticed how many food commercials there were during the program. We members of OA groaned at each one, and empathized with Judy as she was depicted as "starving" for something to eat. One TV viewer (who shall be nameless) said, "I'm on such a strict food plan that I may not even listen to dinner music!"

One 79-year-old Sister, very much like our Sister George Ann, and just about as mobile, has come for evaluation of a gambling addiction. We all feel very sorry for her, but can't help wondering if her community could have found another way of dealing with the problem instead of sending her here, with its inherent difficulties. Everyone tries to be helpful to her, but we cannot be her guardians every minute of the day. 'Tis a quandary!

Another Sister has joined us from a cloistered Poor Clares Convent. It has been interesting and enlightening to listen to the various community stories. One is part of her administrative team in Nova Scotia; another is the sub-prioress of her whole community; yet another is fearful that her community will not permit her to make her final profession if she doesn't receive favorable comments from the counselors here.

Please keep us all in your prayers. Everyone here is suffering in some way, and not all community-members are as kind, loving, and generous as the Racine Dominicans are. Thank you again for all you have done and continue to do for me. I love you all!

Oh, by the way, I'm glad you are interested in my counselor--so am I, of course! If ever there's an opportunity for a "conference lite," I'll inform her about your interest. She's a honey, to tell you the truth. I don't know why I was dreading our meetings. Nothing I say throws her for a loop--and to be honest, a couple times I tried to do just that! ! And sometimes I purposely disagree with her and try to give her a hard time—but something tells me she knows exactly what I'm up to, and she refuses to "play along." Wise woman!

She has a box of tissues handy, and **does not** make fun of me for being a weeper. It's therapeutic to talk to her--I wish the sessions were THREE hours long! Quite a change, I know--but there it is. That, too, teaches me something: Mary, don't be so quick to judge people! Mary, don't allow fear or pre-conceptions to paralyze your reasoning powers or get you in a tizzy! Mary, don't be such a dope! Now if I could only get Mary to listen to all that good advice......

Dear Sisters,　　　　March 1, 2001

What a week this has been! Tuesday for
lunch we were served boiled potatoes and
a turkey hot dog in a wheat bun, complete

ME

with packets of mayonnaise, relish and mustard. I enjoyed the hot
dog, then had an idea when I looked at the pieces of potato.
"Hmmmm,"thought I, "I have all the makings of potato salad except
a hard-boiled egg. I wonder---" And then I asked Yvonne, one of
the servers, if I could have one of the eggs left over from breakfast.

She returned from the kitchen apologetically. "You already had a
protein [the hot dog]," she said.

"Yes, but I'm allowed two," I replied oh-so-sweetly. (I really had an
appetite for potato salad!) Back to the kitchen she trotted. ("Be still,
my heart!" I told myself; "You **might** get your wish!")

An instant later, cold water was (figuratively) dumped on my hopes.
"If we give you an egg, everyone else will want one," she prophesied.

And that's one of the joys of living in a treatment center! I ate my
cold potato in silence.

After the centering prayer service on Wednesday, Sister Mary
Bea's lips were moving; that was the only way I could tell she was
speaking, because her voice is whisper-soft, and my hearing is, after

all, that of a septuagenarian. After a few minutes, I thought I had detected a sentence or two: "If you felt something stirring within you, perhaps you could slip from your chairs and sleep on the floor."

" **WHAT?** " I asked in dismay. Then I learned she had said ". . . perhaps you would like to share on Friday at a quarter past four." (One of the first things I will do when I get home is to have my ears checked!)

Maybe I should have had them checked when I went to the doctor's office the next day. But I was so happy and excited about the visit that all other thoughts were superseded by my joy. For the **first time in my entire life,** a doctor was concerned that I was losing too much weight, too fast! She wants me to lose about a pound a week from now on.

"But, Doctor," I wailed, "then it will take me **forever** to reach my goal!"

She remained firm. "Modify your goal," she said blithely.

They are afraid I am becoming obsessive about my weight, so— although I continue to step on the scale here every Tuesday,--from now on I must not face the right direction: I must stand backward on the scale, and the nurse will tell me my weight only once a month.

Believe me, they have all kinds of techniques to deal with people like me! (I have learned that it was my dear therapist Anne who came up with that solution. That's the way horses are weighed so they won't get "spooked.")

After early rising, a full morning, then craft class for more than an hour this afternoon, I was exhausted. I sat down to read—and promptly fell asleep. At 4:12, I was awakened by a knocking at my door.

There stood Sister G., the Clinical Director. "Weren't you supposed to be at exercise class this afternoon?" she glowered.

"Oh—yes," I replied in a daze.

"Well—why weren't you there?"

"I forgot," I said sheepishly.

"Any special reason you forgot?" she persisted.

"No—I just forgot."

"Didn't you have a schedule?" she asked accusingly.

"Yes," I admitted.

"Well," she said, "now **I'll** have to tell the nurse **and** the exercise instructor **and** your counselor that you *forgot*." She left in a queen-sized huff, and I felt like a worm that had just been trampled on.

And that's another joy of being in a treatment center.

The benefits continue to outweigh the pain, and so I remain at Guest House, trying to "bloom where I am planted." One of the 40-ish Sisters confessed that she had never learned how to pray the Rosary, and asked me to teach her. That will be my Dominican ministry here.

I try to preach by word and example, but sometimes my words are not the right ones, and my examples aren't so great, either. Still, as they keep reminding us, we don't have to be perfect; all we have to do is keep on the path to Progress! I ask your prayers that God will do in and for me what I cannot do for myself.

I am most grateful for your prayers, your good wishes, and your letters and notes. They give me courage during the difficult times (like this week, for instance!)

One of the problems is that--unlike at Siena Center, where there's always at least ONE person to whom you can turn for understanding and sympathy--here there's **no one!** Oh sure, there are lovely, compassionate women in residence, but I don't want to add to their burdens. Everyone here has her own set of problems--some far worse than mine--and how could I go to someone who's already suffering, and moan to her?

Then, too, there's the consideration of loyalty. I feel honor-bound NOT to complain about someone's treatment of me. I don't want to influence another person's opinion of the Clinical Director--or any other member of the staff. I feel the same way about these private incidents as I do about confession: since the confessor has an obligation to preserve the Seal of Confession, then so does the penitent. It's really no one else's business. So where does that leave me?   ALONE and BEHIND THE EIGHT BALL!

But don't feel sorry for me! I'm only getting what I deserve. It's different from life **BGH** (Before Guest House), however. In my previous existence, many people were either a little intimidated by me or a little impressed. . . .and they kept quiet about my objectionable behavior--for the most part, any way.

Here, I am trying to learn how to accept criticism honestly, gratefully, humbly. I'm learning, too, that wearing <u>masks</u> of humility /acceptance /meekness etc. doesn't work! These counselors are **sharp** ! Sometimes I feel as if I'm made of cellophane, because they can see right through me into motivations, ideas, conceptions, attitudes that I haven't yet acknowledged about myself. The downright disturbing thing is: **THEY ARE USUALLY RIGHT!**

(Especially that Anne Sutherland. Either she is one perceptive psychologist or--haha--she's been there, done that--and she knows all the signs!)

Please keep all of us in your prayers. We need them!

Dear Sisters   March 7, 2001

(I am in a very foul, profane, angry mood right now—sorry—if I
don't let out some steam, I will BLOW UP. Then the fire engines
would come, the police, the ambulances, etc. So WATCH OUT:
here it comes. If you can't stand the heat, skip the first part and go
to the 4th page...I'm warning you now!)

I'm going through another trauma this week—wonder if this will be
a pattern from now on? Two weeks ago I handed in my Step Two,
but Anne returned it to me, saying that I should put in more details.
So I inserted more details, bringing it to six pages.

Yesterday she returned **that one** to me, saying, "You are not at
Guest House to demonstrate your skill in English composition!"
When I asked her what she meant by that, she answered that it was
too well written, and I should try for a simpler approach.

Sez I, "I taught English for 52 years. During that time I developed a
certain knack with the written word; writing comes as easily to me
as breathing. It is second nature for me to notice sentence structure,
vocabulary, coherence, transitions, etc. in writing."

"Well," she replied; "just make it simpler. What do you mean, for
instance, when you write 'I abrogated sovereignty of my life to my
addiction'?"

"I meant," I answered, "that I let my addiction have control of my
life."

"Why didn't you just say that?" she queried.

"Because—because-- I had used that expression in a previous sentence," I sputtered.

"**SEE**?" she triumphed.

"Do you want me to condense what I wrote?" I asked. "To omit some parts—the poems, perhaps?"

"No, she answered. "They graphically describe your various states of mind; I feel I know you better because of them."

"Then **what**?" I puzzled. "Do you doubt my integrity, my honesty?"

She responded, "**No**—I believe you are being brutally honest, and what you have here is a perfect Step Two. The problem is, it's **too perfect!**"

"This is the way I write," I claimed. "Do you want me to change my personality? It's as if, although my native language is English, you are now asking me to write in French. Or—' as I looked at a painting of her favorite horse—"you asked someone who has some talent in painting to paint a horse not in his usual style, but as a third-grader would do it. In rejecting my writing, which is a facet my personality, you are rejecting **ME!**" (And you know how intolerably painful that is to me!)

"All right," she conceded. "You **don't have to re-write it.** Instead, record it on a tape-recorder, but without notes!"

Go figure. I'm wondering: If I **refuse** to record it, what can they do to me? I've already done the damn' thing, haven't I? Not once, but **twice!** If she doesn't like it enough for me to present it to the group—Tough bananas! That's her problem, not mine! And besides, she'll discover I'm no slouch when it comes to <u>public speaking</u>, either! As I try to analyze it, she is probably trying to help me overcome my perfectionism. What the hell that has to do with an over- eating compulsion is beyond me. I **like** being a perfectionist; I happen to think we compulsive over-achievers get the world's work done. I **like** being dependable and responsible and correct. Dammit, I know all too well that I AM NOT PERFECT; but some parts of me are fine just the way they are, and I wish to hell they'd leave those parts alone!

Sometimes I feel like an insect squashed between two glass slides being examined under a microscope. I feel naked and vulnerable, all parts of me exposed.....**AND I DON'T LIKE IT!!!!!!!!!!!!!!!!!!!!!!!!!!!!!!!**

Anne, especially, seems to have discovered the keys to my personality, and I couldn't fool her if I wanted to—dammit! She's gifted: intelligent, perceptive, and wise (and almost as **stubborn** as I am!)—an unusual combination in a young (40's) and beautiful woman.

Outside of that I am calm, serene, tranquil, composed, contented, placid, and oh-so-virtuous! Grrrrrrrrrrrrrrrrrrrrrrrrrrr!!!!!

Following is the letter for the more sensitive, protected, shockable Sisters at Siena Center. I don't want to offend them or lead them astray with my inappropriate language. Those of you who read my rantings will, I hope, understand that I had to let off steam—and will not think I am like this all the time!

Henry W. Longfellow described Miles Standish as "a little furnace heated hot in a minute." Well, I'm not "Miles," and I'm not "little," but I am "heated hot." It has taken me three months and one week to reach this point, but right now, I'd like nothing better than to march right up there and announce that I am **LEAVING. I am finished. Done... Kaput. So long, it's been nice to know ya Adios. Aloha...Auf wiederseh'n. Hasta la vista, Baby! Nazdrovia. Au revoir. Ciao.... Good-bye One and All !!!**

P. S. I'm NOT GOING to re-do that Step Two. So there. I'll wait here till Doomsday if I have to, but **I WILL NOT DO IT!**

Dear Sisters,   March 14, 2001

St. Patrick's Day will have passed by the time you read this, but perhaps I will be in time to wish you a Happy St. Joseph's Day and a Merry First Day of Spring. Consider it done!

Dingy little piles of snow still dot the landscape here at Guest House, but there is a promise of warmer days to come in the lengthening days, brighter sunshine, and breezes not quite so bone-chilling. I envy you the sight of the lake, with its waters reflecting the blue of the skies, its rippling waves, its never-ending fascination.

Joan Ebbitt lectured here this morning, mentioning that she had spent some time in Racine with the "dear Dominicans" there. Both she and Sister G. had fulsome praise for the community, saying that the members were open and receptive—really outstanding in both acceptance and understanding. I tip my hat—and my heart—to you!

It is lecturers like Dr. Douglas McDonald, a top-notch physician, psychologist, addictions specialist, who have greatly consoled me by removing the moral stigma I had long associated with compulsive overeating. Accepting it as an illness to be managed rather than as a sin to be atoned for has changed my relationship with God—and with others, too.

I am grateful for the "Irish" stationery and the messages they brought. It is always good to hear from you and about you; your notes brighten my day and ease my loneliness. Thank you! The

Sisters here are kind and congenial, but there's "no place like home," and there are no people like "family."

I now attend three outside-the-house OA meetings every week: two at night, one on Saturday morning. At one of the meetings a man observed that—Caution! If you are likely to be offended by vulgar language, skip the rest of this paragraph!—(Still with me? OK, but you've been duly warned!)-- a man observed that if you stand with one foot in Yesterday and one foot in Tomorrow, you're likely to pee all over Today! And a woman said that she "had decided to <u>turn off</u> her ass-kicking machine."

Isn't it wonderful what OA meetings are doing to expand my vocabulary?

One of the Sisters "graduated" last week, and had asked if it would be possible for someone to present a choral reading of a poem she had found very meaningful: Frost's "The Road Not Taken." I volunteered to arrange the poem for Light, Medium, and Deep voices, printed copies of the arrangement, and solicited volunteers. They performed beautifully, and everyone was pleased.

Well, not **everyone.** Sister **G.**, Director of Guest House, thinks I am doing things just to be in the limelight—primarily to get attention. Next week another client will celebrate with Departure Ceremonies. She asked me to prepare a reflection for the occasion.
(What will **G.** say ? I really don't give a flying fig what she thinks. I am using a talent God gave me. If she doesn't understand, **TOUGH.**)

Remember the development of Ecclesiastes, Chapter 3, presented by the Executive Team last summer? I am trying to do something similar, this time relating it to the Guest House experience:

> A time to plant seeds for healthy, constructive living...
> A time to end self-recrimination, blame, and fear...
> A time to break down walls of silence and secretiveness...

Times like these make me wonder: How do people without a wonderful community ever make it to Recovery? It is no wonder that there are so many relapses—especially among the overeaters. Will power is not the answer; loving support, even confrontation and intervention, combined with the addict's own hard work, holds the key to success, I am learning.

The 79-year-old Sister left after only two weeks; her frail health did not permit participation in the program. That leaves me as the second-oldest again, and when dear B. leaves in a few weeks, I will be The Old Lady of Guest House! That's all right—I'm <u>feeling</u> younger every day! I am even able to ignore the elevator and walk up and down the stairs most of the time. Before you know it, I'll be prancing like a young gazelle!

Please continue to keep me—and all the others here (Sister-patients, counselors, therapists, nurses, housekeepers, chaplains, cooks, servers, maintenance men, drivers, receptionists, etc.)-- in your prayers. Yes, even the **Director**! We all need help so very much!

Dear Sisters   March 21, 2001

It's Spring, it's Spring! I look out my window,
eagerly scanning the skies for flocks of robins to
come swooping by; I closely examine the tree-branches, searching
for signs of swelling buds; I ardently inspect frozen flower beds,
hoping to spy emerging shoots of shy crocus—all in vain!

"Patience, patience!" a small voice tells me. "All in good time, all in
God's time!" So I settle down to serene and tranquil waiting—one
day at a time—for the fulfillment of Spring's promise. I must learn
to be just as patient with God's workings in Nature as He is with me
and my efforts to bloom into renewed life and re-formation.

Even though the crocus and daffodils seem to be lagging a bit
behind schedule, however, there are other signs of warmer weather
ahead. Remember all those Asian ladybugs that descended upon us
last year? Some of them have followed me to Guest House! My
bedroom windows are only a short winged flight from the trees, so
I'd better prepare for an Asiatic horde's invasion.

 While I was brushing my teeth a few weeks ago, I noticed a <u>dimple</u>
that had never before indented my left cheek, then another one on
the right side. *How charming!* I thought. *I'm turning into a 75-
year-old Shirley Temple!* I've been paying close attention, and now
there are <u>four dimples</u> on each side, plus some crawling out from my
eyes and on my chin. *Wait a minute,* sez I to me this morning,
those aren't dimples—**they're wrinkles!** Sigh. It's true. Instead
of Shirley, how about Mrs. Methuselah?

Last week I celebrated my 100th day at Guest House. Since they tell me the first hundred days are the hardest, there'll be nothing but clear sailing from now on! (**I hope someone tells Anne that!**)

Dear Anne is getting tougher on me. During her lecture last week, she ignored my raised hand and did not call on me, although she called on people alongside, ahead of, and behind me. After three attempts I finally got the message and kept my hand down. I told the Sisters about winning $100 in the SCHS calendar raffle, and they asked me what I would do with it. "Donate it to the missions," I replied. "I don't really need anything except a helicopter to get me out!"

I've been feeling bad because Anne returned my 8-page paper on the Second Step because, she said, it was "too perfect." "You have not come to Guest House," she said, "to demonstrate your skills in English composition!" Even when I protested that I had learned something about composition after teaching English for 52 years, she still insisted that I change my style and re-write the paper in a more simple way. So what can I do? I have learned not to argue with her. (She always wins, anyway.)

Someone remarked—facetiously, I hope—that one month is added to a client's stay every time she disagrees with or questions a directive. Nevertheless, I am still hoping to be discharged sometime before my hundredth birthday.

So I've been told to write Step Two for the **third** time--not **write it,** exactly, but to give my answers into a tape recorder--answers to a stupid high-school-level workbook on the behaviors of compulsive eaters. I felt so angry, hurt, rejected, and humiliated that I had made up my mind that **I would not do it!** But this morning, after Group, I was going up the stairs when Anne came up right behind me and asked, "Mary, what are you doing?" I answered (very coldly--DUH!) "I'm walking up the stairs, Anne, going to the second floor."

"Oh no, you're not!" she insisted. "You were dizzy yesterday. I love you, and I don't want you to take a chance of dizziness recurring while you're on the stairs." Then taking my hand, she said, "I love you, and I am going to take you on the elevator with me."

Alleluia!!! Alleluia!!! Alleluia!!!

Did you hear that??? She said she **loved** me!!! So the icebergs in and around my heart all suddenly melted away; I went up to my room, got out the tape recorder, and spoke the answers to the lovely, lovely, **lovely** workbook lessons.

Resolution for the Future: I will be simple. I will not be complex. I will write in easy-to-read sentences. See Mary write. Write, Mary, write. Oh, look. Look and see. Mary will write one more paper. (Please pray that Mary will also learn how to accept criticism humbly and graciously.) God bless you and your patience with me!

Dear Sisters,   April 1, 2001

I've just finished composing an Introduction to
our Holy Thursday liturgy. May I share part of it with you?

*The musical "Jesus Christ, Superstar" shows us a tormented Jesus
in the Garden of Gethsemane, weeping and crying out to God in
agony. We addicts have known similar agony. We hold it in our
hands now, mystically joining it to the suffering of Christ. During
this liturgical celebration, we expose our communal woundedness
to the merciful compassion of our God. We ask God to look upon
our frailty, to accept our brokenness and sanctify it as Jesus'
suffering was sanctified—for the salvation of all humanity.*

*In this commemoration of the Last Supper, we unite with Christ
and His priests down through the ages as we joyfully, gratefully
acknowledge our share in that priesthood. With unconditional love
and deep humility, we have "priested" each other. Not with sacred
oils have we been anointed, but with the sanctified and sanctifying
tears of our Sisters. Wounded healers guided by the Spirit, we
have ministered to each other in ways beyond the world's
fathoming. And, with hearts brimming with love and gratitude,
we now—as a community—praise God for blessing us, entrusting
us, with pain—allowing us to share in our humanness the price of
His vulnerability.*

The others in the committee have said they will decorate the altars,
bring in the plants, arrange for the washing of feet, etc. if I will do
the writing.   Of course I agreed!   Among the intercessions I

included: **"That through faith, we may be able to discern God's presence not only in the Eucharist, but also in our own addictions, we pray..."** I wish all the counselors, especially dear Anne, could hear the part about being "priested" by the tears and confidences of others. I think <u>they</u> heal us by their ministrations more than confessors do.

It's always a delicate subject to speak of faith or religion, however, especially if they are not Catholic. I wouldn't want to offend anyone. These writing illustrate my state of mind right now, and I thank God and the ministries at GH for helping bring me to these realizations. I am learning valuable lessons for the rest of my life. My motto for this past week has been: *Instead of thinking yourself into a new way of acting,* **act** *yourself into a new way of thinking.*

Guess what? Last Friday I joined a group of others and went to a health spa for aerobic water exercises. I struggled valiantly against my fear of water, and actually moved various body parts exercising— in the **shallow** end of the pool, of course. I eventually grew bolder and walked the full length—clinging desperately to the railings along the side. Wonder of wonders: the pool did not overflow; neither did anyone run away screeching in horror at the sight of me in a bathing suit!

I'm beginning to enjoy our Tuesday and Thursday exercises, too. I do what I can for a few minutes at a time, and am growing stronger and more limber. I have even discovered hip bones that I had never before been aware of, generously padded as they are!

I've had some rough times lately, and have been near total discouragement and depression. Please keep me in your prayers; I promise all of you a remembrance in mine. I can't tell you often enough how much the hope of your prayers and understanding mean to me.

Some of the clients here do not tell anyone--even family members or members of their own religious communities that they are in a treatment center because they are suffering from an addiction.

Some times when the subject comes up, I openly admit that I keep in touch with all of you, and that I honestly relate some of the challenges I have faced. I do not understand how a woman can keep her sanity and sense of balance without communication with those who have been close to her for years--even decades.

It's true that not all communities are as open as ours. But if they are interested in maintaining good health among community members, wouldn't you expect them to keep informed about all kinds of "health"--mental, emotional, physical, spiritual? If we were angels we wouldn't need to learn much about psychological problems; but we are only human, with human needs and human weaknesses. We learn here at Guest House to admit our own frailty, our brokenness. They do not keep us from God, but can draw us even closer.

I have found great peace in admitting that I need God and I need others; that I am not perfect or even close to it, but with St. Paul, I can rejoice in my infirmities, be glad of my emptiness, because then the Power of God can come and fill me with all the Good, the True, the Beautiful that God is. But it is only when I am willing to let go of my own selfish concerns and relinquish all to God that I make space for Him. And it is in giving all else up that I ready myself to receive the One Perfect Love that will unite me to Himself.

So: THREE CHEERS FOR GOD, and another cheer for God's entrusting me with one of His favors--an addiction!

Easter Sunday, Alleluia!

April 16, 2001

We are an Easter people, rejoicing in the glorious Cross of Jesus, Alleluia!

Dear Sisters,

Very special greetings to all of you, and deep gratitude for your welcome messages on that beautiful Easter stationery, or even scribbled on an old paper bag, for that matter! I appreciate each one. I took the whole pack to Jesus in the Blessed Sacrament during my vigil time on Holy Thursday evening, and asked Him to bless every one of you.

Some highlights of the past week: After a communal Penance service, Father Jim anointed each one, saying: "Remember, O Christian, the day of your Baptism, and open your heart to the Holy Spirit."

On Holy Thursday, although we were prepared to have a resounding *Gloria* with chimes, bells, and various musical instruments, Father <u>forgot</u> to intone it!

On Holy Thursday night, while several of us were in the Music Room with the Reposed Blessed Sacrament, tremendous wind storms set off the fire alarm; we had to extinguish the candles, grab our coats off the rack, and scurry outside, where we moaned and shivered until the "All Clear" was announced. (Health centers are required to conduct fire drills at least once a month, during the various employee shifts. We hope this one suffices for April.)

Our liturgical observance of Good Friday had to wait until 6:30 PM because Father Jim was helping in a neighboring parish during the afternoon. In his homily following the reading of the Passion, Jim said, "We have done the absolute worst thing we could have done— we laid cruel hands on the Son of God and put Him to death. Yet that was not enough to lesson God's love for us. God's love exceeds even that atrocity."

Saturday morning—believe it or not—we had to keep our regular schedule and ride 45 minutes to Warren for a meeting. Overeaters there were extremely concerned about how they would keep their food plans on Easter, when everyone seems to celebrate with delicious food. We at Guest House are freed from that temptation— nary a jelly bean dares to cross the threshold! And certainly not even a crumb of chocolate!

(In class one day last week the instructor was warning us about the danger of misunderstandings once we rejoin our communities. "What will you do," she asked, when someone starts making comments about what you have on your plate?" MG, a kind, loving, amiable cloistered Dominican, muttered under her breath, "Bump 'em off!" Hearing that gangster phrase from her gentle lips undid me, and I had a giggling fit that just wouldn't quit. In imagination I saw her with a machine gun, taking aim at all 28 nuns in her community, "bumping them off" one by one!)

Here I'm taking advantage of your good will, enclosing this poem, "At Emmaus," in my letter. I hope it will touch you.

Now nearing its goal at Emmaus is the journey I started alone.
Along the way, such wonder—how swiftly the years have flown!
Companions, friends, have eased some pain of loneliness by caring,
By loving words of comfort, remembering, and sharing.

O'er rugged roads and craggy steeps, past fields of velvet green,
By waters rough or smooth as silk—what splendid sights I've seen!
Yet through it all, a Presence dear, a Spirit, gently dwelling
Within my heart, within my soul, with peace beyond all telling.

In broken Bread and given, I see pierced hands extending
In Eucharistic, saving grace: Love's Sacrifice unending.
My searchings ceased at Emmaus; my yearning heart then knew:
Christ, You are my love, my life, my all. My journey ends in You.

At Emmaus I recognized Your Love, Lord, in Breaking of the Bread
You took my heart, my very life, and gave me Yours instead.
Stretching Your arms in welcome, You brought me to Your side;
Weary wanderings over, in You I now abide.

I love this holy season, and exult in every **"Alleluia!"** I have persuaded the Sisters with whom I attend morning Mass to include an Easter hymn every day during the Octave. "All right," they agreed, "but YOU have to start it!" We may be hitting the bottom of the scale next week, but at least it will be festive! If all else fails, I can play a recording of the "Hallelujah Chorus"! I thank you again for all your prayers, your words of encouragement and support. I am indeed blessed to have such a caring community, and I thank God for each one of you. May the Risen Savior enfold you in His peace!

Dear Sisters,   April 18, 2001

I'm hoping to dispel some feelings of major depression by writing to you. When I return to Siena Center in spirit, seeing you in chapel for Mass or in the dining room for meals, it restores a sense of peace and happiness. The memory of your kindness eases my heartache.

And why does my heart need easing? I was on the "Hot Seat" yesterday in the presence of about 30 women: the Clinical Director, the Nurse, the Spiritual Director, 3 Therapists (including my dear Anne, who blushed furiously at one point—she was **so angry** with me!), and more than 20 clients.

A few clients who tried to defend me were quickly, summarily squelched; everyone else appeared to agree that I am **independent, argumentative, critical, stubborn, self-willed, controlling, manipulative, and that I "want-what-I-want-when-I-want-it."**

You want to know the worst part? They're **right**! Wanna know the best part? They don't know the <u>half</u> of it! But it was hard to take, nonetheless.

I went for a long walk around the grounds after I was publicly humiliated and nearly guillotined, and saw places I had never noticed before. "Lookout Point" sticks an inquisitive nose out into a small lake where a bright blue rowboat arches its back to the sky. I thought of climbing in and rowing out, but there's no outlet—I would just have to go 'round and 'round. No relief in that

Nearby, a large mural depicts an angel telling Tobit, "Fear not; I am with you." I answer, "You jolly well better be, because I surely need help from somewhere!"

Today's Gospel told of Mary's mistaking Jesus for the gardener. In a way, she was right: God is a gardener of our souls, and very carefully tends what has been planted, offering sunshine and rain as each is needed. I won't complain because this seems to be my rainy season.

Sunshine will be headed my way in mid-May when I'll be having dear visitors from Racine. I wish they could fill a bus and bring a crowd! Instead, please keep up your prayers for this flawed Sister of yours. I've heard that "You can't teach an old dog new tricks"; but this mangy old dog is certainly going to try to learn new attitudes and ways of acting!

Please be patient with me as I share a few of my problems with you. I know each one has her share, and my times of trouble can't compare with some of the crosses you bear. May a merciful and compassionate God bless us all!

P. S. One of the "old-timers" here just told me that when a client is confronted as I was, her reactions are noted and analyzed. If she goes around with a long face, acting moody or vindictive or shamed out of her gourd, that's BAD NEWS. But if she bounces back with energy and resolve, that's GOOD.

Well, I can't promise about "bouncing back with energy and resolve," but I will do my best to act normally, and not let one big humiliation vitiate the good things I know have been happening with me. I am a difficult case--mostly to myself. I am my own worst enemy. No matter what anyone else can say or do to me, I have done worse things to myself.

PS #2. Anne just knocked on my door with an appointment for next week. She asked me if I'd like one during <u>exercise</u> time. I was flabbergasted. "You'd do that for me?" I asked in astonishment. "Of course!" she said. **That dear woman!**

See--that's what I mean. And that's typical of the way things work around here. Let's say Client XYZ smokes in her room (a NO-NO) and sets her bedroom afire. Fire alarm sounds, everyone has to get out--everything stops while firemen do their thing, finally give the OK to return. XYZ gets called in to the Clinical Director's office; all the counselors, therapists, nurses go there too. XYZ gets told off, bawled out plenty, hears lots of incriminating stuff about her disobedience, selfishness, stubbornness, arrogance, pride, etc. etc. until it comes out the wazoo--and then some. Finally, after an eternity or two, XYZ is allowed to apologize, to promise to make amends, resolve NEVER to do it again--and the meeting is over.

Then, as they are all leaving, what do they do? Continue the meeting? Continue to berate XYZ? Say nasty things to her or about her? Shame her, denigrate her? Destroy what little self-confidence she has left? **NOT ON YOUR LIFE !** Everyone goes on about her business, no recriminations, no re-hashing, no second-guessing, no blaming or scolding or lecturing..... It's all been taken care of. Period. Finished. Life goes on as before.

It really reminds me of the forgiveness of God when we sin. Once He forgives, He doesn't ever bring it back up again. It's over--for good! That's the example they give here: You made a mistake. OK. Did you learn from it? Good! Now let it go.

WOW! I've never experienced anything like it in my life! That alone is worth 6 months at Guest House!

P. S. No--no one has ever--as far as I know--set fire to GH!--Just in case you wondered!

Dear Sisters,   April 22, 2001

This used to be called "Low Sunday," in contrast to the high
solemnity of Easter the previous week; now it is known as "Mercy
Sunday," and I rejoice with you in the merciful compassion of our
God.

Thank God my personal storm is over, and I am once more basking
in the sunlight of hope. Not without a price, however! My poor red
nose bears mute testimony to a tearful period. The tissues we have
here are one step removed from tree bark; lotions and salve have not
yet repaired the damage. But soon I may resemble the Easter Bunny
more than I do Rudolph of Reindeer Fame.

MB, who has been a supportive member of the OA group at Guest
House for nine months, will be departing this week. She asked me
to take care of the "entertainment" portion of the ceremonies, and I
decided to recruit Sisters who would do a dramatic reading of Act III
of <u>Our Town.</u> The one who is to read the part of Emily has a
southern accent; when she reads *That's all they are—blind people!*
It sounds like "<u>blond</u> people," so I'm working with her on
diphthongs. I told "Emily" that it was her job to make me cry.
"Pooh!" she scoffed. "That's not hard at all!"

I went to the pool again Friday, and was actually brave enough to
walk in the perilous depths of the center, which is all of FIVE AND A
HALF FEET deep. Of course MG was holding my left hand; J was
holding my right; I was wearing "water wings" and clung desperately
to a floating board—but I did it. And we didn't encounter a single
shark!

I hope you understand my use of initials. I have learned that we must honor confidentiality at all times; we are not to divulge other clients' names or communities or anything about them. Visitors here are cautioned not to ask personal questions; if the client chooses, she may give facts about herself, but no one may presume to ask.

In spite of the admonition they had received, two retreatants eating in our dining room answered my request to join them with, "Yes, you may sit at this table—if you tell us your name and addiction.!"

I won't tell you what I <u>thought,</u> but I responded sweetly, "I'm Lizzie Borden, and I'm a compulsive hacker!" We went on to have a friendly—albeit impersonal—conversation.

Have I told you that we are allowed to rent (with Guest House paying the fee) two or three videos every weekend? I've seen more movies here in four months than I did in the last six years! Last night we viewed "The Green Mile," about which I had heard and read many good reviews. But I resisted it because I claimed that prison movies don't appeal to me. Was I ever mistaken! Although the setting is a prison, and some language is harsh, the over-all impression is one of great spirituality. I recommend it to you. One more excellent film is "Philadelphia," with Tom Hanks in yet another great role.

May I share with you an excerpt from "The Big Book" which I was directed to memorize:

Acceptance is the answer to all my problems today. When I am disturbed, it is because I find some person, place, thing, or situation—some fact of my life—unacceptable to me, and I can find no serenity until I accept that person, place, thing, or situation as being exactly the way it is supposed to be at this moment.

*Nothing, absolutely nothing happens in God's world by mistake. . .unless I accept life completely on God's terms, I cannot be happy. I need to concentrate not so much on what needs to be changed in the world as on what needs to be changed in **me** and in my attitudes.*

That's a mouthful, isn't it? I am trying to learn that very valuable lesson.

However--what if you had a job to do, and the job absolutely required a piece of special equipment which you could get without paying a penny. But you had been told you could not leave the house. What would you do? Would you--like me--consider it was using your God-given reasoning power and initiative, and ask **someone else** to get that equipment? Or would you get your knickers in a knot because **I did ask** a person who was more than willing to do the favor?

I am presently *persona non grata* because I asked my cousin, Sister Theresa, to get a book from the library for me--a book of classic literature containing Wilder's play, Our Town. The ensuing fuss made me think they expected a pornographic novel or some incendiary piece of radical anarchy with which I would work for the downfall of everything good, holy, and worthwhile. Or perhaps a do-it-yourself recipe book about how to make chocolate fudge without sugar, chocolate, flavoring, butter, and other ingredients forbidden at GH. But a play recognized as a classic? 'Tis a puzzlement!

Saturday will mark the four-month anniversary of my acceptance into this program at Guest House. I have changed in some ways, but I am still working at knowing myself and doing something about the less admirable facets of my character and personality. Believe me, it's easier to lose the fat than it is to lose certain other habits! Don't expect a miracle of perfection, however! I am coming to realize it is a life-long journey, with many detours, pitfalls, relapses, and turn-abouts. I am grateful to be making that journey with you.

I continue to be most grateful and appreciative of your concern, support, and encouragement. The road is long, and the way is lonely. Did I read that somewhere, or is it my heart speaking? No matter—thank you for your kindness and love.

April 29, 2001—Feast of St. Catherine

Dear Sisters,

I am with you in spirit as we celebrate our special day. God's Providence has separated us temporarily, but I walk the corridors of Siena Center and rejoice with you in the presence of our Sisters and Brothers. I know that they, too, are experiencing the joys of your hospitality and kindness.

I hope your weather is as pleasant as ours. The grounds are beautifully green and velvety; forsythia bloom in golden profusion; a few trees (apple? cherry? peach? pear?) are decked in delicate pink or bud with a feathery mist surrounding them like a halo. The little lake, ponds, and fountains bubble, gurgle, and spout in rhythmic patterns—

I hadn't even finished that last sentence when another Sister came in asking for assistance with a letter she was trying to write. Of course I helped her, and then listened for two hours while she poured out her heart about her problems.

This stay at Guest House has alerted me to a whole segment of our Catholic community that has never before occupied a prominent place in my prayers: addicted priests and religious. Besides the problems caused by various addictions, there are added the feelings of guilt and betrayal of a holy vocation, the shame that accompanies what one perceives as a violation of the vows etc. For the rest of my life I will pray for addicts of all kinds, especially for priests and religious. I hope some of you will, too.

Before I was interrupted, I was telling you about the beautiful grounds here, with grass, bushes, and trees giving us delight. Animals, too, bear careful watching. There is a herd of about 16 deer that make their home here. They seem to be aware of the "No Hunting" signs, and are grateful for the food put out for them daily. It is fascinating to watch the young ones trail hesitantly after the doe, trusting she will lead them aright, while the proud buck stands majestically tall, overseeing their progress. Sisters tell me that a family of goslings has taken up residence near one of the ponds; sand cranes scratch around in another sector; squirrels, raccoons, and possums conduct interdenominational services; and a skunk or two announce their presence in unmistakable fashion.

Then there are the wonderfully vari-colored two-legged creatures who saunter, stroll, jog, roam, promenade, march, hike, tramp, lope, or just walk around the grounds—some jubilant or exhilarated, others meditative or reflective, still others glum or depressed. No matter what the mood or stride, we <u>walk</u>. I thought I had gone at least 5 miles the other day, but the others told me the distance to the gate was less than ½ mile. I am trying to condition these old legs so they will be able to take me around Siena Center in the not-too-distant future!

Life here continues in the same routine, except for an occasional break. Our reading of <u>Our Town's</u> Act III was well received by our visiting retreatants, with moist eyes discernible in quite a few listeners. The leaders and head nurses of communities interested in treatment for their Sisters gather for a kind of instructional retreat periodically here at Guest House.

The retreat is called "Walking With the Wounded" (that's us: the addicts) Some of the clients--who still hurt from less than kind treatment from their leaders and / or communities-- call the meetings "Stomping All Over the Wounded."

"Walking" or "stomping," they nevertheless enjoyed our emotionally moving presentation, with its themes of appreciating life—even the most ordinary kind—every moment; of trying to see others as they are, in all their beauty; and of believing that we are   connected— even in death-- to those we have loved.

 Anne S. was not here (intentionally, I believe, because of the "Battle Royal" we had about my using a bit of initiative to get a copy of the book I needed for the script. I think I already mentioned that, didn't I?) And G. did not betray by the slightest twitch of an eyelash that she was happy about the performance or because of the praise we received from the visitors. But that's typical of her, and I don't need either her or Anne's approval to know that it was good!

I have learned—through the presentation of more than 40 plays during my career—that everything good—I mean really good—has a price one must pay. If I suffer during the rehearsal and pre-production stages, I am certain that the venture will be successful. And the more I suffer, the better it turns out! I wonder if others have experienced the same thing.

Tuesday two more Sisters will be leaving, with several planning therapeutic leaves in May and June. The rest of us experience impatience, envy, and frustration as we await our turn.

At present I am working on Step Four: "a searching and fearless moral inventory" of my life. It is difficult enough writing all the negative things; giving an account of the positive ones is even harder. Step Four is like an all-encompassing, universal General Confession. Thank God it is NOT presented to the whole group, but only to the counselor—who probably knows it all anyway!

I thank you for the notes, letters, and messages of all kinds that you send me. It was difficult to hear of the deaths of Sisters Annette, Loretta, and Mary Chris, and not be present to bid them farewell.

May God grant you a happy spring, with flowers, birds, and buds of all kinds to cheer you and remind you of new and vibrant life. Keep us in your prayers, and know that you are ever in mine.

May 6, 2001

Dear Sisters,

Greetings on a beautiful spring day! Though the outdoors is inviting, I must stay here and work on my Step Four: "a fearless and searching moral inventory." I have four categories to work on: Anger and Resentment; Fear; Shame and Guilt; and Warmth, Love, and Kindness. Under each category I am to have four columns, delving into and examining past feelings, motivations, fears, ways of dealing with frustrations, evidences of self-centeredness, arrogance, sense of self-worth, etc.

And so on. It's very difficult for me, because I must go back so far and dig up all those negative emotions. On my list of "favorite things to do on a bright spring day," this occupies about the 3,400,000th place!

A Sister of Charity here received word yesterday that one of the members of her community—one of five ministering in Guatemala— had been shot and killed by men who wanted her beat-up old car. Evidently things are in a very confused state there, and the government has little or no power to stop such wanton acts of violence. Other Sisters have been attacked and harmed several times already, but this is the community's first death. *R. I. P.* How I admire those dedicated missionaries! Some of the clients here are or have been missionaries, and I marvel at the depth of their love for the indigenous people they have served so willingly and so well.

I missed Mass this weekend because the priest scheduled to preside at Saturday evening's liturgy failed to show up. The others went to a neighboring parish this morning, but I was "grounded" and unable to leave the house. You see, I have been dizzy with severe headaches all week; on Friday, as I was climbing into the van, I blacked out a moment. It took two men and the nurse to get me into the wheelchair. As I was being wheeled back to my room, I lost my lunch—and my breakfast—and dinner from the night before—and everything since last Thanksgiving, it seemed!

Diagnosis? A severe Meniere's attack, which also resulted in a fall early Saturday morning—no broken bones, just bruises—and enforced inactivity for the entire weekend. Even now, I'm still headach-y and more dizzy than usual, and I have to wear dark glasses because the light hurts my eyes.

I'm wondering how the clinical director will react to them tomorrow morning at our group session. Last Monday when I closed my eyes a moment, she said sharply, "Mary, open your eyes! You look as though you're falling asleep over there!" Whatever else may be said about life at Guest House, it's never dull!

At present there are only 13 of us here, with the two now on therapeutic leave hoping to be discharged later this month. At my last meeting with Anne, my therapist, she actually said the words "therapeutic leave" to me, so I'm hoping that I may be returning to

Siena Center for a week in June. Then—if all goes well (according to a questionnaire to be completed by certain Sisters) I may be able to start planning for my departure. **WOW!**

I have mixed feeling about that. Of course I want to return to Siena Center, but I am fearful, too..... fearful of what all of you will expect of me, and fearful of how I will respond to temptations from which I have been mercifully spared for six months. There are some things about Guest House I know I will miss...and some of them are the very things I dreaded when I first came here.

I remember saying very seriously to Sister G., "I understand that the Sisters gather in a group periodically and discuss the troubles they experienced as they dealt with their addictions."

"Yes, that is correct," she answered non-committally.

"Well," I continued, "I just want you to know I will not be doing that. You see, I am a very private person, and I don't readily share such things with others."

"I see.," she answered amiably.   I wonder if she smiled when I left her that December day....or did she shriek hysterically?

I also dreaded conferences with Anne. Now---I wish I could put her in a large trunk and take her with me to Siena Center---or have her move to Racine and set up a practice there. I would be her constant client!

And how I will miss the camaraderie of the other clients! We have been privileged to experience a beautiful community here, with a loving understanding, loyalty, acceptance, and mutual concern. I have never experienced anything like it outside family life, and I thank God for all the blessings these women have brought to me!

As of today, I've lost 51 pounds. More importantly, I am experiencing a new level of confidence in myself; I am aware of a certain balance in my emotions; I have learned much about addictions in general and compulsive eating in particular, and I have a better understanding of how to control my triggers and urges. I realize that I will have this addiction all my life, but I realize, too, that I am not alone—that God can and will help me to do what I cannot do for myself. I also realize that I can and must ask others to help me manage this life-long struggle...one day at a time.

All things considered, the gain has been worth the pain!

You know, an extended time like this has been extremely beneficial for me, and I honestly wish everyone could have an experience like it. We go on our way for years at a time without a break, or with only a week's retreat and a week's home-visit. I can speak only for myself, of course, but the home-visit is not really a time of rest and relaxation: too often it has been one dinner or lunch or "party" after another, meeting relatives or friends we haven't seen for years, trying to "catch up" with each other's lives.

A retreat, too, requires 2 or 3 days to get rested; another 2 or 3 days to become truly immersed in the theme of the retreat--and then it's over. But 6 months at a place like GH presents one with the opportunity to delve deeply into oneself, and examine the motivations, practices, ideals, dreams which prompted us to join this community in the first place. To examine, to compare, to evaluate--all this takes time.

Another gain has been the proven support of my community. You, dear Sisters, have made it possible for me to undertake and persevere in this program, and I am deeply, lovingly grateful. I thank you with all my heart! I don't want to lose this trust in you and your kindness, this relationship which my acknowledgement of vulnerability has made possible. Therefore, I ask you in humility and acceptance, please keep me in your prayers and in your concern. I want to be a vital and productive member of our beloved community. Please help me along the way to progress. God bless you all!

Dear Sisters,   May 13, 2001

We were without a priest again this weekend, so some of us attended Mass at Christ the Redeemer Parish this morning. The pastor is an aesthetic- looking man, thin to the point of emaciation; I thought a strong gust of wind would surely blow him away. But when he started singing in a rich baritone and then preached with power and fervor, I had to revise my preliminary impressions in a hurry!

In a masterful manner Father Daly correlated the Easter season, liturgical readings, Mother's Day, and the morality of capital punishment—quite a feat! He had a parishioner read Julia Ward Howe's Proclamation to Mothers, written in 1870, calling upon mothers of our country to denounce war and violence; urging women to stand firm in supporting Christian love and forgiveness— all the gentler virtues they had taught little ones at their knees. Then he led us in singing "The Battle Hymn of the Republic," which Howe had also written. It is no wonder that many of us stopped in the entryway after Mass to sign the petition against capital punishment.

Last week our darling resident guru, Dr. McDonald, lectured on the recent Newsweek article dealing with the innate capability of the brain for contemplation. **"Our greatest power," he said, "is to surrender our helplessness to the Omnipotence of God, to be open to union with the Infinite."** He went on to comment on the Rosary. "Whoever thought of it," he remarked, "must have been a genius, so to engage the right side of the brain with fingering the beads and repeating the words—while the left side of the brain is left free to soar to the heights of contemplative prayer." Until recently, Dr. McDonald stated, some monasteries in the Russian Orthodox Church forbade the monks to recite the Rosary unless they had received prior permission from their spiritual directors because it was considered such an exalted form of prayer.

I am eagerly anticipating Tuesday and Wednesday, when the Sisters from Racine will be here. I will not mail this letter, but will ask them to deliver it instead—it should arrive even faster by OP Transport!

The other clients have been teasing me, asking what they should say about me to those who visit. So far, we have gone through about half of the alphabet with "therapeutic adjectives" amid many side comments and much laughter: A: accepting; B: balanced; C: compliant; D: diminishing; E: energetic; F: fair; G: goal-oriented; H: honest; I: intrepid; J: jocular; K: kind; L: loving; M-----And there they got stuck. Words such as *managerial* or *maniacal* were rejected as not "therapeutic" enough. (We were <u>almost </u>stymied by D; when someone suggested "docile," I retorted: "Wait a minute—this has to be at least <u>somewhat believable!</u>")

Some of the clients have gone to visit the Detroit Zoo this afternoon. I am not particularly fond of seeing animals in captivity, so another Sister and I will be movie-goers, seeing "Bridget Jones' Diary." I have read that it is a modern version of Jane Austen's <u>Pride and Prejudice,</u> so I hope it will be enjoyable. Guest House pays our admission price, for which we are both grateful.

(**Later:** Poor Jane must be whirling in her grave at the vulgarization of her genteel, charming novel of manners. This movie is a travesty of it! The one good thing about it is that at different times and in different circumstances, the hero and the heroine are able to tell each other in total sincerity: "You have some terrible faults, and there are things about you that I do not admire. But I like you *just the way you are."*)

Tomorrow morning, instead of our regular classroom lecture, we will meet in chapel for a session with Sister Mary Bea, the spiritual director. MB will conduct a "Grief and Loss Ritual" with us to help resolve various issues in our lives: from loss of control over our addictions, loss of trust, grief of being away from our own convents and Sisters, grief over loss of loved ones, loss of abilities etc. It brings tears to my eyes just to think of all the ramifications. I hope plenty of tissue-boxes will be provided!

I can't tell you how your messages of support and encouragement have cheered me this past month or so. I saved many notes and re-read them when I feel depressed or discouraged. It helps to realize that I am not alone; that someone believes in me and is praying for me. Thank You!

I look out of my window towards Wisconsin and see a beautifully full lilac bush, a lavender cloud of fragrant blooms. I wish I could send some of the perfume your way. You'll have to take the wish for the deed, however, as I send you assurances of loving appreciation for all you have meant to me. May God, Who moment by moment makes all things new, keep renewing our spirits according to the mind and heart of Christ.

My Life History

(With emphasis on   my addiction of compulsive eating)

My maternal and paternal grandfathers were alcoholics, and both Mary Darga and Edward Fischer, suffering from the effects of having alcoholic fathers, had promised themselves never even to date anyone who drank. They found in each other the kind of loving, devoutly Catholic spouses they sought. I was the first child of Mary and Edward,   20 and 22 years old respectively, at the time I was born. Although my father, grandfather, and other relatives spelled the surname with a c, the doctor recording my birth omitted that letter, and so all my life I have been c-less.

I was born on January 6, 1926, more than three-quarters of a century ago. My mother slipped and fell on the bottom step of the basement stairs, and I was born prematurely, delivered by my Grandma Darga and immediately baptized as Grandma held me over the bathtub. I was so small and puny that it was feared I would not live.

As the first child of the new generation I was petted, pampered, and spoiled. My mother taught me variation of a song popular at the time, and I remember being delighted when I was asked to perform, singing, "Mommy and me, and Daddy makes three / We're happy in my Blue Heaven."

My paternal grandparents were farmers from Germany; the Dargas were factory workers from Poland. Both families lived on the East Side of Detroit, within walking distance of each other. Because Grandpa Darga had died four years earlier, and Grandma could use help around the house, Mom, Dad, and I—and 15 months later, a baby brother, Tom—lived with Grandma Darga, a quiet, generous woman who had suffered much both physically and emotionally because of her alcoholic husband, who had assumed little if any responsibility for their twelve children.

Grandma Fischer, too, was warm, loving, generous, open, and kind. Grandma was a large-boned woman, who had quit school at the age of eight because her parents deemed her big enough to work in the fields. In her prime, she weighed more than 300 pounds, but no one complained because being hugged by her was like being enfolded in a warm feather quilt. Grandpa Fischer, on the other hand, was a cold man, angry, moody and truculent—we were afraid of him and his sister, Great Aunt Mary, also an alcoholic. I remember being frightened once at a family gathering when both Grandpa and his sister went on a rampage, frantically searching cupboards and closets for liquor which they thought was being hidden and kept from them. Even as a child I had seen and heard enough about the ravages of alcohol so that I was never tempted to drink.

Food, however, was a different matter. Both grandmothers, my mother, and all my aunts were excellent cooks, and the house was continually fragrant with the tantalizing odors of pies, cakes, doughnuts, cookies. "Eat, eat," each one would say when we came to dinner. "Have some more potatoes, ham, beef, *kruczchicki, gawumpki, psadnina (Please excuse my phonetic Polish). . Ja chen kocham.* I love you; have another piece of pie." Or: "*Wie geh'ts? Vas ist los?*" What's the matter? You don't like my German Chocolate cake?"

Neither Mom nor Dad smoked or drank, but they both loved food, especially sweets. After graduating from school, Dad found a job in a bakery, where he was happy meeting people—and being treated to the merchandise. He was fired because the boss caught him giving doughnuts an extra portion of jelly. From there he moved to a position as a salesclerk in a grocery store, eventually becoming first a butcher, then the manager.

By the time my sister Christine was born in 1929, Mom and Dad owned and operated a corner grocery store. We lived in the back of the store, which was kept immaculately clean. I remember darting in and out of the living quarters to fill my pockets with candy which I filched from the window cases when my parents were busy with customers. When I discovered that my coat pockets were torn and that anything put into them fell down to the bottom of the lining, I made continual trips back and forth to the candy counters. I remember my mother's asking in exasperation, "Why do you wear that coat all the time?"

Around this time, when I was five years old, I had an experience that I have never forgotten, but about which I have never spoken. Dad was in the store dealing with customers; four-year-old Tommy was "helping" Dad; Mom, pregnant with Barbara, was in bed dealing with severe pains. It was the day we expected our "insurance man" to come and collect the premiums.

Mom had given me some money in an envelope and a little receipt book to give to him, and I was proud and happy to be entrusted with an important task. When he came, he sat as usual at the dining room table. My impression at this time is that he was a middle-aged, portly man who wore glasses and whose hair was thinning, but I'm not sure if that description is accurate, or if I have fashioned it from a conglomerate concept.

While he was at the table, I stood opposite, observing his actions. After a while, he said, "Come over here, Honey, I'll show you something."

I shyly went to stand beside him, and he showed me the numbers he was writing in the receipt book. Soon he put his right arm around my waist and told me I was a pretty little girl, and he' d like to hug me. I always liked being hugged or kissed because it made me feel special, so I said "OK." and smiled at him.

But he didn't really hug me. Instead, he took his arm away from my waist and reached under my dress, under my bloomers, and started caressing my bare buttocks.

That frightened and alarmed me; I jerked away and ran to Mom's bedroom, where she was asleep. I stayed there until the insurance man left.

I don't know why I never told Mom or Dad about this incident. Maybe I felt it was somehow **my** fault; I don't know. I felt "funny" about it—a new kind of feeling I couldn't describe or share. However, a handful of candy would make those strange feelings disappear. But to this day, I feel "funny" if someone touches me unexpectedly.

In these later years, I have felt guilty because I let him get off free, free to molest other little girls. I should have told someone, but I didn't. Instead of telling about it, I soothed troubled thoughts with candy. The supply of candy was cut off, however, when Mom came into my bedroom one day and saw my cache of sweets spread out on my bed, while I stood gloating over it.

My raids on the candy displays, I was sure, were the cause of Mom and Dad's losing the store. The Great Depression may also have been responsible. Dad had given credit to the people asking for it. I remember the little credit books with the dark green covers. Dad kept them in a box, hoping, I suppose, that some of the people would eventually make an effort to pay their debts. No one ever did, unfortunately. But my brother Tom and I practiced our addition on the sums in the books. "Why did you keep giving the people credit when they didn't pay?" I asked Dad once.

"What was I supposed to do?" he answered. "They were hungry, and there was food in the store. I couldn't turn them away."

I realized later that such an attitude was typical of my generous, kind father whenever he heard of someone in need. We lost the store and our home—but all I could think of was losing the constant supply of candy.

This was the beginning of very dark financial circumstances in our home. Dad would go out looking for work, asking if he could paint walls, put up wallpaper, clean attics or basements, do **anything.** Mom said later that it was a good day if he came back with fifty cents for a day's labor. She fed her family potatoes and milk, milk and potatoes, with an occasional piece of meat for Dad.

I missed my sweet treats. Once, when I was given a dollar to buy bread (10 cents a loaf) and milk (10 cents a quart) and a T-bone steak for Dad (25 cents), I spent the rest of the money on candy. I remember sitting on the curb greedily devouring the chocolate, then making sure that my face and hands were clean before I returned home. I told my mother I had lost the money. And I watched her cry.

In spite of those financial worries, however, I never heard my parents complain, never heard any word of complaint or even worry. They simply kept on doing the best they could do without making a fuss about it. I remember watching Dad repair the soles of his shoes with pieces of rubber he had salvaged from the scrap pile at work. He traced the outline from his old shoes, then glued on the new piece. But **his** were the only shoes he repaired that way. When anyone needed new shoes, somehow we had the money to buy them.

Once I asked my Dad about the old furnaces I remembered from some of the houses we lived in.   I told him I remembered how periodically he'd have to use a shovel and get the ashes out, then haul them somewhere.

"Dad," I asked, "how did you keep our homes warm? I don't remember ever being cold."

"Well," he answered, "I figured that a warm house would prevent some of the sicknesses going around. I didn't want anyone in my family to suffer and get sick, so I always made sure we had a good supply of coal and the fire was kept alive."

"What about at night, though?" I asked.

"I got up around two o'clock every night and went down to check the furnace." Dad answered matter-of-factly.

"You did!" I exclaimed, stunned. "Gee—Thanks, Dad!"

I was so pudgy that when I received my First Holy Communion as a second-grader, my mother bought me a two-way-stretch to wear under my pretty dress, and I shamefully realized for the first time that my appearance was not acceptable, that I was different from the other little girls who marched with me.

Other children in school teased me: "Fatty, Fatty, two-by-four/ Can't fit through the kitchen door." But I retaliated by excelling in all my school work. When teachers singled me out to go up to the 8th grade and show off my reading skills, or recite Patrick Henry's speech in front of the classroom, I felt I was paying the other kids back for their tormenting remarks. "Nyeah, nyeah" I would think arrogantly, "I'm fatter than you, but I'm also smarter!" I learned angrily defensive, aggressive behavior to deflect the hurt others caused me.

When I was in the fourth grade, I was chosen for the lead in the annual Thanksgiving play, to be presented before the entire school and all the teachers, with parents and friends invited. I was ecstatic, and ran all the way home to tell Mom about it. She was very happy for me, and promised to help me learn my lines.

We worked together on the script, Mom helping me declaim with expression and good projection. Within a week I had memorized all the lines and the actions, gestures, and positions recommended in the script. I was ready to wow the world with my dramatic abilities!

Then the box of costumes was delivered to our classroom: the pilgrim women and girls, the men and boys, the Indians—all were scheduled for specific times for fittings.

The day for my fitting started out like an ordinary one. But it ended with a hurt unlike any I had ever known. There was no costume big enough for me. Some other girl would be given the part. I was to turn over the script to her.

And I sought comfort from such loyal friends as candy bars, ice cream, and extra helpings of desserts.

Every once in a while I overheard my mother expressing concern over my weight. "Don't worry," kindly relatives would say. "That's just baby fat. She'll grow out of it when she reaches her teens." When I heard that, I resolved that when I reached my teen-years, I would stop the compulsive over-eating I had been engaged in. But all too well had I learned that desserts—especially chocolate—made me feel good, made me forget my schoolmates, made me oblivious to the scorn of my father.

Even though I was large—very large—for my age, I was still troubled by a malady usually associated with small children: I was bothered by nocturnal enuresis: I wet the bed. Mom was sympathetic and patient with me because her own mother and two of my uncles had had the same condition. But Dad thought that I was just a fat, lazy slob—too careless to get up at night. I know that Dad loved me— loved his whole family: he worked and sacrificed so much for us. He thought he was doing the right thing in shaming me; in reality, he was helping to erode my feelings of self-worth. But I tuned out his angry, sarcastic taunts by using my allowance to buy sweets.

In addition, extra pieces of cake and pie were used to comfort me, my brother and sisters when we felt sick, to reward us for good grades, or even to bribe us into good behavior. "If you behave yourself when we go to Grandma's," we children were told, "we'll get ice cream on the way home."

I had a generally tolerant attitude toward my brother Tom and sisters Christine (3 years younger than I) and Barbara (almost 6 years younger). Tom, only 15 months younger than I, was a typical boy, I suppose. He had his bike and his friends and pretty much did his own thing. At the time, there was a brand of canned sauerkraut called "Silver Floss" on the market. Since my name was Florence, I was subjected to a variety of nicknames: Flo, Flossie, Flow-rinse, etc. But Tom knew how to really irritate me by calling me "Silver Floss" —because I knew what a sour, mean, smelly person I was.

oChristine taunted me about my bed-wetting, even telling some of my classmates about it, and I was angry with her—and hurt—for a long time. Tom, on the other hand, denied I had such a problem when some acquaintances asked about it. I was grateful to him.

I remember walking to Midnight Mass with Tom on Christmas Eve when I was 14 and he was 13. That was the first time, I think, that we really spoke to each other on a friendly, almost-adult basis, and I realized that he was a pretty good guy! The years have served only to re-enforce that observation, and I am proud of my dear #1 brother!

I was envious of Christine. She was attractive—and THIN—and she and Barbara wore pretty dresses. In addition, she was lively and had plenty of friends, while I had one—maybe—and only because I tutored her. It was later, when we were both mature, however, before I really came to appreciate her goodness, affability, and generosity. We were very close as adults, and I grieved deeply at her sudden death from a car accident.

I felt very maternal toward my sister Barbara, almost six years younger than I. Because of financial straits, Mom had to find a paying job to help support the family. That meant Barbara, too young for school, stayed with Grandma Darga during the week, returning home on Friday evening, then going back to Grandma's on Sunday.

I'm afraid Barb and her siblings were almost strangers, although we all loved her quiet, considerate ways. I am sure none of us realized what she was thinking or experiencing as she switched from one home to the other. I am so glad and grateful the years have brought us a sisterly closeness that has been a wonderful blessing in my life. She is a loyal friend, a wise counselor, and a constant joy to me.

During summer vacations back in the 1930's, I looked after Barbara while Mom and Dad were at work, and took great pride in her progress and success. I introduced her to the local public library, and helped her withdraw six books one summer afternoon. A few hours later, she had read all the books, and I took them back, telling the librarian, "My little sister read all of these in one day!" It had not occurred to either one of us that one could read and enjoy the same book more than once, or share a discussion about it. We were busy making trips to the library that summer.

I enjoyed ironing Barbara's little dresses (telling Christine that she was old enough to iron her own!) and getting her ready to go with Dad to meet Mom and drive her home from work. I washed her, combed her hair, and delighted in the sweet smell of her.

None of my siblings was affected by sweets as I was. I saw Barbara take one piece of chocolate—when she could have had a handful— and marveled. I saw Christine pass up a piece of cake or pie because, as she said, she was "watching her figure." Even Tom, pudgy for a few years, exercised and played ball so much that he was able to maintain a healthy weight. Only Mom, Dad, and I seemed to have eating problems.

My parents and all of Grandma Darga's children were devout Catholics. Religious pictures and crucifixes had honored places in their homes, and sometimes vigil lights burned before a picture of the Sacred Heart as a sign of prayers for some special need. We would never think of missing Sunday Mass or semi-weekly confessions.

I always felt that it was Mom who was responsible for our religious up-bringing. She loved her own mother so much that in gratitude to Grandma's teachings and example, Mom patterned her family life in imitation of what she herself had experienced. I have been grateful all my life for that.

But whatever Mom did, it was handled subtly. Rarely if ever did she raise her voice at us or scold. Instead, her hurt and disappointment at some kind of offense made us feel worse than if she had threatened us, as Dad did, with: "I'll wrap you 'round a pole!" Once in a while, though, she took out her wooden mixing spoon and gave a parting swat to whoever was darting away.

She was a Sweetheart of a Mom, gentle, loving, good-humored, sensitive, perceptive—I could go on and on. She was quick to praise, to encourage, to express interest in our lives and activities. I loved to finish my Saturday chores early so I could help her in the kitchen. There I learned not only how to cook and bake, but many of the values that she espoused. I learned other things from Mom, too— songs that she taught me so we could sing together, bits of poetry, stories, remembrances of her early life. Most of all I learned **love** from a wonderful, generous, great-hearted woman of valor. I still miss her every day.

Dad, too, was a person of principle. Once, after having just learned it during religion classes, I told my Dad that Sister said if a person had to work on a Sunday, he or she was not obliged to go to Mass on that day. Dad had been in the practice of rising around 4:30 on Sunday mornings for early Mass at a monastery whenever he had to work that day. I'll never forget his answer: "I don't go because I **have to;** I go because I **want to!**"

I believed him because I thought he was a good man. I had never heard him use the name of Jesus or God irreverently; he never cursed or swore; despite his probably inherited propensity for alcohol, he indulged very seldom. When he opted for early retirement at the age of 62, a friend gave him a bottle of spirits. When Dad died 23 years later, there was still liquor in the bottle.

After his dreams of owning and operating his own store were destroyed by the Depression, he had finally found work at the U. S. Rubber Company, building tires—a difficult job requiring constant attention and being subject to reeking, obnoxious odors. He told me once that he hated the disgusting, stomach-turning smell, and felt that no matter where he was, he always felt that the air was polluted by the stinking stench of burning rubber—This from a man who loved the fresh air of gardens, and never wanted to work indoors!

He and the others who worked at the same job would take a heavy piece of already cut rubber, lift it up on the press, hold the press over it a specified length of time, then take the hot, half-pressed piece, toss it over on its other side, and hold the press down again.

Some friendly old hands at the job told Dad, "Hold the press down for 15 seconds, while you count to 20: One thousand one, one thousand two..." Dad followed the instructions for a while, then said, "I'm not going to waste my life **counting**! I'll ask the priest for a prayer I can say." He was delighted when he discovered that praying half of the "Hail Mary" for the pressing worked just fine. He prayed the second half while he was tossing the rubber on its other side in preparation for the second pressing.

Every Friday—"pay day"—he brought home either bakery or candy from Sander's, a favorite in the Detroit area, and we all feasted.

When I reached my teen years, I tried to quit my mis-use of food during times of stress— but I failed again and again. I couldn't figure out why, when school work was so easy for me, it was so difficult for me to stick to a diet. I **knew better.** But knowledge wasn't enough when it came to diets. And I tried them all: the grapefruit diet, the banana diet, the eat-as-much-as-you-want-as-long-as-it-is-only-one-food diet etc. None of them worked **because I eventually cheated** on each one! My parents spent money they could ill afford on visits to doctors who helped neither my enuresis nor my compulsive overeating.

Finally, after a special novena to St. Jude Thaddeus, Patron of Hopeless cases, my mother took me to a specialist who had just moved to Detroit. This urologist found that although I was large, my bladder muscles were those of a three-year-old; furthermore, my bladder was—and still is—less than half the size of an average person's. After a series of painful treatments, the problem seemed solved.

That meant that I could proceed with my desire to enter a convent and become a Sister. From the time of my First Communion I had felt that God was calling me to belong to Him in a special way, and I had talked to my mother about it. She said that she and Dad wanted me to be happy, and if that was what I really wanted, they would help.

I know relatives and friends were surprised when I announced that I planned to ask for entrance to St. Catherine's Convent in Racine, Wisconsin. I certainly was not the stereotype of the teenager who entered a convent. I was, of course, inordinately fond of food; I was crazy about movies and movie stars (I had seventeen scrapbooks about Don Ameche !) I would rather read than engage in any activity. My "nose is always in a book!" my Dad had complained. I was fourteen years old, and I weighed 210 pounds—and I was interested in joining a convent!

I was not noticeably pious; though I loved Holy Scripture, especially the New Testament, and memorized many beautiful passages that I could repeat when I was alone. Jesus Crucified was my great love, and with a heart full of compassion I often put myself at the foot of His Cross and poured out my heart to Him. Of course I didn't tell anyone about this—it was our private communion. I was drawn to a life of inner quiet and contemplation, though I thoroughly enjoyed good times with fun and laughter, too.

In addition, I had achieved academic recognition from my school work and from tutoring others. That seemed to be the area in which I would find my niche, and I associated "teaching" with "Sisters," since they were the only teachers I had ever known. The Sisters had always been kind and encouraging to me; they seemed like admirable women leading the kind of life in which I could be happy, so I decided I would join them. On August 30, 1941, I joined a group of seven young women who rode the train to Racine, Wisconsin, the Motherhouse of the Dominican Sisters. (Of course as I have matured, I have developed other motivations for living the live of the evangelical counsels.)

When I returned home for a vacation the following June, my relatives exclaimed to my parents, "You're not going to let her go back, are you? It's obvious that she's not happy—she's lost so much weight!" I had lost 60 pounds without even realizing it, without trying to lose. I was happy: convent life agreed with me; I was accepted and liked—and I lost weight.

But a year later, when adolescent hormones manifested themselves and I began experiencing strange new yearnings and emotions, I resumed overeating in an attempt to deal with them. For years I tried to bury such feelings under a load of food. Giant strides have been made in the last fifty years regarding an understanding of and appreciation for human sexuality. In those days, however, confessors refused to discuss problems relating to chastity, advising me to seek counsel from my superiors; superiors told me it would be a "mortal sin of curiosity" if I wanted to know more than the basic facts of life; spiritual writers told me things like Augustine's "If your eyes light upon a man, let them never be fixed upon him"; and Francis De Sales' "First comes looking, then admiration, then lust."

I began to feel I was sinful and depraved,   unworthy to be in the presence of holy women who never had such problems. If I wanted to stay in the convent, I was sure, I had to squelch all such thoughts and not pay attention to feelings, emotions, and sinful curiosity. One superior had me mark a calendar with a big black **X** all those days when I had shown any emotion. So I ate to hide all my depravity and shame, some days feeling I would explode with frustration, loneliness, and a desire to love and be loved.

Yes, I knew that God loved me. But I needed someone with ***skin.***

Many years of my religious life were spent in this way, trying to sublimate or deny problems, always wearing a mask of gregariousness while hiding personal doubts and difficulties. Eventually good confessors and directors helped me deal with my sexuality, but I have always had trouble along those lines.

Once I heard a story about a young Novice who experienced such problems. "When will it end?" he asks his youthful superior. "I don't know," the young priest answers. "Let's go ask Father Prior." The two of them approach the middle-aged Prior, soliciting his reply to the question. "Sorry, Brothers," the Prior confesses, "I don't know when it will end." So they go to the sixty-year old Abbot, who tell them he doesn't know either. Next they ask advice from a weak octogenarian. "Well, boys," the old man answers, "be sure you let me know if you ever discover the answer. That particular monkey has been on my back all my life!" I used to think the story was wildly hilarious. Now I think it is not a bit funny.

I have always been a good teacher--competent, efficient, conscientious—so many and various assignments were given to me. After a while I felt I was being used as a dray horse, being loaded with more and more work until I felt my knees would buckle under the burden. I remember sitting on my classroom floor one night sobbing with agony, wishing I had enough money to run away. I thought I would take a bus someplace—anyplace—as far as the money would take me. Instead, I took a box of 24 candy bars— and ate all of them.

Fifty years ago a doctor, unaware of the possible danger of amphetamines, prescribed Dexedrine to help me lose weight. I lost weight, but irreparably weakened my heart. Dr. McDonald has assured me that a week on Dexedrine now would kill me, and I believe him.

In 1969, after 25 years of teaching in junior and senior high schools in Wisconsin, New Mexico, and Michigan, I applied for and was granted a graduate teaching assistantship for doctoral studies at the University of Cincinnati, which meant that I would live in an apartment near school, take courses, and teach. I thrived on that regime. I was happy in the academic environment, fulfilled emotionally by friendships formed, and delighted in apartment living. I lost weight gradually and safely and reached a satisfactory weight for me, about 185 pounds.

For 27 years I taught in colleges and universities in Ohio, Wisconsin, and Michigan, enjoying every class, feeling alive as I thrilled to the challenges, grateful for the opportunity to help form young minds and characters. Occasionally, however, when stressed, lonely, or frustrated, I resorted to compulsive overeating of sweets. I loved to cook and bake, loved to entertain friends and relatives at meals and parties. Then, after they had gone home, I treated myself to all the left-over desserts as a reward for being such a good hostess. Sometimes I made myself sick, and had to call the university to cancel classes for the next day.

Probably the most important project of my life started when I began to care for a dear friend in 1982. A Dominican priest, he had been my teacher, confessor, and spiritual director before succumbing to multiple strokes. Severely brain-damaged, he had been confined in turn to eight different nursing homes and a mental institution, and had become bitter, lonely, and suicidal; finally, after another stroke, at my request and with the Provincial's permission, he was discharged to my care on December 8. The doctor told me, "Just make him comfortable. He will not last till Christmas." I sent to New Orleans for his habit and cappa, and made some preparations for his funeral.

He was like a six-foot baby: incontinent, uncommunicative, helpless. I learned how to feed him through the gastrostomy tube inserted into his body, how to do other things I had never done before. I was also teaching full-time at the University of Michigan at the time. It was unutterably difficult—and I welcomed every minute. I felt that I was loving and being loved. (Our mutual motto had always been **Love Serves.**) Gradually he improved. Once he said, "God will reward you for the good care you give to me." I remember answering, "I'm not so sure. I learned that you get a supernatural reward only if you have supernatural motivation. And I'm taking care of you because I love you." "You wouldn't love me," he replied, "if you didn't love God first."

I found that very consoling. All the while I ministered to Bob, I had no problems with food because I was happy--though exhausted— and I knew I had to take care of myself in order to take care of him.

Illnesses came, but not through any fault of my own. I had neither the time nor the inclination to binge on anything, though I longed for rest!

The doctor had said Father Bob wouldn't last till Christmas. But he hadn't said **which** Christmas. I cared for him for 12 years, until he died in my arms on May 21, 1994. I haven't stopped grieving for him yet; sometimes at night I hear him calling to me for help. "You're lucky you still have a good mind," one doctor told me, "Because your body is going to pot!" I have undergone surgery more than 24 times because of illnesses or conditions related to my poor eating habits: gall bladder problems, rectal tumors and ulcers, hiatal hernias, inguinal hernias, heart attacks, mini-strokes, congestive heart failure etc.

Ill health forced me to retire six months past my 70th birthday and to go to our Motherhouse, Siena Center, in Racine, Wisconsin. In losing my health and relinquishing my profession, I felt that I had also lost much of my identity as a person and as a contributing member of the community. I also lost the verve and vitality that had colored my life and my teaching.

Angry with God, with myself, with the whole world; resentful and depressed, I turned to food for consolation. Because of intestinal problems caused by overeating, there are many foods I could not tolerate, but there was always an appetite and longing for sweets. I frequently binged on cookies and milk—undoubtedly a throwback to childish ways and preferences. I have been known occasionally to flaunt my intelligence, but I certainly have been moronic in my eating habits! In the 4 ½ years since I retired, I had gained more than 60 pounds.

When, in October, I hit 280 pounds, with the 300-mark just a hair's-breadth away, I was shocked and dismayed. "No wonder," I thought: no wonder I had heart problems, breathing difficulties, lethargy, chronic fatigue, arthritic pains throughout my body. Some people are so stubborn that they have to hit a brick wall before they confront their addictions. The 280 was my brick wall. I asked my superiors if I could come to Guest House. They were ecstatic, and facilitated my move.

I personally contacted the 110 Sisters living at Siena to tell them of my eating disorder, my futile attempts to deal with it, and my decision to turn the problem over to God and to Guest House. They have been most supportive, understanding, and encouraging. One of them said, "I never knew you had a problem of any kind. You always walked around so confidently, smiled so readily—Now you are showing us a few chinks in your armor!"

I think no one would have dared to suggest such a move to me—I am not known for either humility or meekness—and they were all glad that I was finally wise enough to take the first step for myself.

I am glad for myself, too, because I realize the depth of my problem more than anyone else ever could. I realize and admit, too, that often I hide behind an arrogant, cynical attitude which alienates others. I am afraid to allow others to get too close to me, lest they discover how flawed I am. I pretend to be someone I am not: the know-it-all with encyclopedic knowledge, omniscient and infallible.

My pride mirrors the sin of Adam and Eve, wanting to be as God. I regret and deplore this attitude and renounce it. However, somehow, I cannot resist hiding behind it occasionally, especially when I am hurting.

But here I am, willing to cooperate with my Journey to Wellness, eager to take every step that will bring me closer to my goal.

COPY

June 15, 2001

Dear Anne Sutherland and the Clinical Staff:

It was with cautious optimism that I requested a therapeutic leave several weeks ago. Now, having further experienced the concern, support, and encouragement of both the staff here and my community members at Siena Center, I feel prepared to ask for a discharge from Guest House.

Of course, I have conflicting emotions about this. Part of me feels hesitant and apprehensive, even as another part sends signals of hope and assurance. I feel I have taken a few uncertain "baby steps" on the Road to Recovery. . . .

Through lectures, conferences, group therapy sessions, Overeaters Anonymous meetings and associations, I have been strengthened and empowered to make positive changes in my life-style, to live more fully as my true self. Practice with the tools and skills of recovery has given me a new level of confidence in myself and a growing sense of trusting acceptance of others. I have been given a second chance: the power to enrich my future life, to learn how to get in touch with and manage my emotions.

Best of all, I have felt a renewal and re-consecration of my spiritual life. My relationship with God has reached far beyond the philosophical and theological verities on which I relied in the past. My stay at Guest House has encouraged me to experience the unconditional unchanging love of God—to accept it, to rejoice in it, to treasure it.

For all this I am most grateful. Each one of you has played a part in my halting progress, and I thank you. I hope you will at least occasionally remember me in your prayers; I promise you a sincere remembrance in mine.

I will also continue to pray for the success of Guest House's ministry, and for the vulnerable women who come to you for help. May God bless us all!

Sincerely yours,
(Sister) Mary T. Fisher, O. P.

Occasionally

A Beneficent Providence
permits paths to merge, to meld
in harmonious synchronicity.
I thank you for your kindness
in allowing me to share
a portion of your journey,
and for your blessed presence
in a part of mine.
If I have said more than I should,
let your love for me delete
the superfluous;
if less, let my love for you,
as day follows day,
fill in the blanks.

www.ingramcontent.com/pod-product-compliance
Lightning Source LLC
Chambersburg PA
CBHW031828090426

42741CB00005B/174